FLESH AND SPIRIT IN CONFLICT

Practical Studies in Galatians

FLESH AND SPIRIT IN CONFLICT

Practical Studies in Galatians

by Theodore H. Epp

*Founder and Director
of Back to the Bible Broadcast*

$1.50 each

order from

BACK TO THE BIBLE BROADCAST

Box 233 Lincoln, Nebraska 68501

25,000 printed to date—1968
(8219—25M—68)

Printed in the United States of America

FOREWORD

Correct doctrine and practice must be joined for the Christian to mature. The one without the other is inadequate. In these expositions on Galatians there is a happy blending of both. A strong foundation of doctrine is laid and the application made to the life so that the believer in Christ can learn to please God in his daily conduct. Those who hunger for a life of victory over the flesh will find here how to appropriate the spiritual weapons that lead to victory.

These messages were first given over the international radio network of Back to the Bible Broadcast. Many listeners testified of the spiritual benefits received from them. We trust God will enlarge their outreach through their use in the literature ministry of the Broadcast.

—John I. Paton
Literature Editor

CONTENTS

CONTENTS

CHAPTER ONE

AN IMITATION GOSPEL

In both Letters to Timothy the Apostle Paul warned of the religious confusion that would prevail toward the end of the present age. He stated in I Timothy: "Now the Spirit speaketh expressly, that in the latter times some shall depart from the faith, giving heed to seducing spirits, and doctrines of devils" (4:1). In his Second Letter the Apostle predicted that the latter times would be marked by a moral breakdown, false religious claims and widespread deceit (II Tim. 3:1-13). These are the days in which we now live.

It is not to be surprised at that old heresies which confronted the early Church are again being taught by persuasive and eloquent false teachers today. The old Galatian heresy that tried to remove the stigma of the cross by adding Law works to the grace of God is once again spreading confusion among Christians. Contributing in no small way to the success of these false doctrines is the lack of thorough Bible study among many of God's people. Large numbers of them are not clear with regard to what the Bible teaches concerning salvation. This makes it necessary for us to restudy Paul's Letter to the Galatians in order to find the divine antidote for that ancient heresy that seems so reasonable to the mind of the unsaved man and, sad to say, to the mind of the untaught Christian.

There are some things in life that make little or no difference to any of us what we know about them or what we think about them. This cannot be said, however, for subjects relating to salvation which have tremendous bearing on the behavior of men and women and their ultimate destiny. It is imperative that we who are Christians know what is included in the salvation Christ wrought for us. This can only be de-

9

termined by learning what the Bible says. "Thus saith the Lord" must be both our foundation and our guide.

A False Gospel

The Apostle Paul went right to the heart of the problem in the Galatian church when he wrote: "I marvel that ye are so soon removed from him that called you into the grace of Christ unto another gospel: Which is not another; but there be some that trouble you, and would pervert the gospel of Christ" (1:6,7). These Galatians had received the gospel of Christ and then through listening to false teachers had begun to follow "another gospel." The gospel Paul preached had to do with more than ideals, it had to do with a Person. Paul made it very clear that only those who trust in Christ are genuinely saved since only His gospel saves. There are multitudes of people who believe they are right with God, though they are not trusting in the true gospel but in an imitation. They are not born again. The Galatians received the genuine gospel then removed from it to an imitation one.

An imitation is something that follows a pattern but is not the original. It is a model or a copy bearing a resemblance to the original, but it is not the real thing. The imitation is synthetic rather than real. The word "genuine" on the other hand, comes from a root meaning "to beget or be born." It is something "belonging to, or proceeding from." In other words, it is authentic, real, true, pure, genuine, free from hypocrisy and pretense.

Today we have more imitations of things in the natural world than at any time in known history. Some Bibles, for example, are bound in genuine leather. Others look like they have genuine leather binding, but the material is a plastic. We are told that many of the so-called diamonds used in costume jewelry today are actually made of some kind of plastic.

Some of the imitations or plastics in the natural world can be very good substitutes, but such is not the case in the spiritual realm. To be an imitator instead of a genuine child of God is serious in the extreme. The imitator wants to follow the Lord Jesus Christ as an example, professing to believe in some of the ethical principles that Christ so clearly stood for and so ably presented. But the imitator is not born again which is necessary for one who is genuine.

The language used by Paul in which he speaks of "another gospel: which is not another" is on the surface confusing. The puzzle is cleared up for us, however, when we find out that Paul used two different Greek words that have been translated "other" and "another" in the English text. One word is "heteros" which means "one of another kind." The second word is "allos" which means "one of the same kind." So, when we give full play to these meanings we find Paul saying to the Galatians, "I marvel that ye are so soon removed from him that called you into the grace of Christ unto a different kind of (heteros) gospel which is not another (allos) of the same kind." Paul marveled that these Christians had so soon accepted a "gospel" which was so different in character and kind from the real gospel that it had no right to the designation "gospel" at all.

These Christians, after having been on the correct route had taken another route which was leading them out of the way entirely. They had not taken one which was "just as good" but one which was detrimental and wrong.

Genuine vs. Counterfeit Money

Our government produces paper money which is used in exchange for goods. This is genuine money, not imitation. We have to be constantly on our guard, however, against imitation or counterfeit bank notes. These counterfeit notes are "heteros" notes. They are of another kind. They are bogus, not genuine. So it is in the religious world. There are persons who are offering a counterfeit gospel. The Devil, is of course, back of this movement and comes as an angel of light hoping to deceive us. But this counterfeit gospel is not a gospel at all.

A silver dollar and a paper dollar (before the withdrawal of the former from circulation), had equal value in a money transaction. The silver dollar was one of the same kind (allos) as the paper dollar. But there is no such thing as one gospel as good as another. There is only one true gospel and anything else is in error.

The analogy of the counterfeit money and the counterfeit gospel holds true in another sense. The counterfeit or "heteros" dollar lacks government endorsement and its use is a criminal offense. Just so the counterfeit gospel not only lacks God's endorsement but comes under His curse, His anathema. This is why Paul says in Galatians 1:8,9: "But though we, or an angel from heaven, preach any other gospel unto you than that which we have preached unto you, let him be accursed. As we said before, so say I now again, If any man preach any other gospel unto you than that ye have received, let him be accursed [let him be under the anathema of God]."

It is one thing for a person producing and passing counterfeit money to be punished by a government. It is quite another matter for us to fall under the judgment of Almighty God for holding to a counterfeit gospel. The true gospel is totally centered in Jesus Christ. Salvation is in a person, not an ideal. It is not a reward for good behavior though it produces good behavior. Yet behavior does not produce this gospel. Only God can do that and He centers it in Christ. We read in John 1:12: "But as many as received him, to them gave he power to become the sons of God, even to them that believe on his name." Peter taught the same truth to a group of people who had embraced another kind of gospel in his day: "Neither is there salvation in any other: for there is none other name under heaven given among men, whereby we must be saved" (Acts 4:12). It is not by imitating Christ that men are saved but by trusting in Him, because He Himself is the very Life of the believer.

This is clearly brought before us in I John 5:11,12: "And this is the record, that God hath given to us eternal life, and this life is in his Son." God does not give us eternal life apart from His Son. We do not receive it by following a set of good ideals or whatever else we may think. We must receive into our hearts the Person of Jesus Christ. The Scripture goes on to say: "He that hath the Son hath life; and he that hath not the Son of God hath not life." Concerning this salvation Paul later says in Galatians 2:20: "I am crucified with Christ: nevertheless I live; yet not I, but Christ liveth in me." So we participate in His death, for we are crucified with Christ. We are identified with Him in His resurrection, because we are not only crucified with Him but we also live through Him. We partake of His life as the verse teaches: "Though I live, it is not I but Christ who lives in me."

A real, genuine Christian is not one who merely imitates the life of Christ. In fact that is an impossibility to us because Christ's life is a perfect life and we are imperfect. God will have nothing in heaven that is imperfect. The only way we can have perfection is by allowing Him who is perfect to be our life. So when we trust Christ, God sees us not as we are by nature but as we are in Christ. We are accepted in the Beloved. There is no substitute for Christ or for His gospel.

Severe Words

Paul used severe language in addressing the Galatians. This in itself indicates the serious nature of their change in beliefs. He wrote: "But though we, or an angel from heaven, preach any other gospel unto you than that which we have preached unto you, let him be accursed. As we said before, so say I now again, If any man preach any other gospel unto you than that ye have received, let him be accursed" (1:8,9). These are indeed very severe words but the occasion demanded them.

In chapter 3 the Apostle said, "O foolish Galatians, who hath bewitched you, that ye should not obey the truth, before whose eyes Jesus Christ hath been evidently set forth, crucified among you? . . . Are ye so foolish? having begun in the Spirit, are ye now made perfect by the flesh?" (3:1-3). The severity of these words indicates Paul's concern for real truth, the truth we find in the Bible. It is truth which deals with time and eternity and concerns all of us. It is not to be taken lightly. There are many false ideas floating around with reference to salvation, such as how we are saved and how we are kept saved. Consequently, in view of the perils which threaten men when truth is violated or changed, Paul had to speak out.

It is not uncommon for a person to say, "I am sure I'll get there. We're all going to the same place; we might go different ways but in the end we'll all reach heaven." The big question is, "What does the Word say?" That is the important matter. It is not what men think but what God has said that counts.

The error Paul refuted in the churches of Galatia had two forms. First of all, there was the teaching that obedience to the Law is mingled with faith as the ground of the sinner's justification. Then there was the second line of error to the effect that the justified believer, that is the person who is saved, is made perfect by keeping the Law. In speaking of keeping the Law we are making reference to human works of righteousness. It has reference to doing instead of being.

It is no wonder, then, that the Apostle Paul lost no time in getting to the point in this letter he wrote to the Galatians. It was after a brief introductory statement that he expressed his amazement of their defection from the faith. In verse 6 he wrote, "I marvel that ye are so soon removed from him that called you into the grace of Christ." He looked on their defection from Christ and from God's grace as an extraordinary thing. So it was with severity mingled with compassion that Paul wrote to these Christians.

God's Anathema

The following quotations are from the Amplified Version and clarify for us some of the matters we are inclined to gloss over. "I am surprised and astonished that you are so quickly turning renegade and deserting Him Who invited and called you by the grace (unmerited favor) of Christ, the Messiah, [and that you are transferring your allegiance] to a different, even an opposition gospel. Not that there is [or could be] any other [genuine Gospel], but there are [obviously] some who are troubling and disturbing and bewildering you (with a different kind of teaching which they offer as a gospel) and want to pervert and distort the Gospel of Christ, the Messiah [into something which it absolutely is not]. But even if we or an angel from heaven should preach to you a gospel contrary to and different from that which we preached to you, let him be accursed—anathema, devoted to destruction, doomed to eternal punishment!

"As we said before, so I now say again, If any one is preaching to you a gospel different from or contrary to that which you received [from us], let him be accursed—anathema, devoted to destruction, doomed to eternal punishment! Now, am I trying to win the favor of men, or of God? Do I seek to be a man-pleaser? If I were still seeking popularity with men, I should not be a bondservant of Christ, the Messiah" (1:6-10). There is nothing mild about these words. The situation called for this kind of warning and reasoning.

See now how his statements in chapter 3 take on new force in the language of the Amplified: "O you poor and silly and thoughtless and unreflecting and senseless Galatians! Who has fascinated or bewitched or cast a spell over you, unto whom—right before your very eyes—Jesus Christ, the Messiah, was openly and graphically set forth and portrayed as crucified? Let me ask you this one question: Did you receive the (Holy) Spirit as the result of obeying the Law and doing its works, or was it by hearing [the message of the Gospel] and believing [it]?—Was it from observing a law of rituals or from a message of faith? Are you so foolish and so senseless and so silly? Having begun [your new life spiritually] with the (Holy) Spirit, are you now reaching perfection [by dependence] on the flesh? Have you suffered so many things and experienced so much all for nothing—to no purpose? if it really is to no purpose and in vain, Then does He Who supplies you with His marvelous (Holy) Spirit, and works powerfully and miraculously among you, [do so on the grounds of your doing] what the Law demands, or because of your believing and adhering to and trusting in and relying on the message that you heard?" (vv. 1-5).

Paul speaks out yet a third time when he says in chapter 4, verses 8-11: "But as that previous time, when you had not come to be acquainted with and understand and know the true God, you [Gentiles] were in bondage to gods that by their very nature could not be gods at all—gods that really did not exist. Now however that you have come to be acquainted with and understand and know [the true] God, or rather to be understood and known by God, how can you turn back again to the weak and beggarly and worthless elementary things [of all religions before Christ came] whose slaves you once more want to become? You observe [particular] days, and months, and seasons and years! I am alarmed [about you] lest I have labored among and over you to no purpose and in vain."

But Paul's words are not all severe. He mingles gentleness with severity. It was with a tremendous plea from his heart that wrote to them: "My little children, of whom I travail in birth again until Christ be formed in you, I desire to be present with you now, and to change my voice; for I stand in doubt of you" (Gal. 4:19,20). Though he had to warn these believers, they were still to him his little children. Tender words indeed! What these Christians had done had brought great pain to his heart. He had deep concern about their spiritual well-being.

They had not failed in their behavior. They were conducting themselves well. The peril was much deeper and graver than that. The very foundation of their salvation and of their spiritual life was threatened. And if the foundation went, the whole superstructure would fall.

Some years ago when we were adding to our present building at the Broadcast, the builder dug for a basement right up against another building adjoining our property. It was discovered that the foundation of the old building was crumbling. One false move could have brought it toppling into the hole just dug. So it was necessary to undergird and rebuild the foundation of the neighboring structure before we could continue with the new one. This was what concerned Paul about the Galatians. The very foundation concerning the truth of salvation was being undermined. In his Letter to the

Corinthians the Apostle stated emphatically that Jesus Christ was the only foundation. But here were believers in Galatia tampering with that spiritual foundation to where spiritual life and eternal destiny were threatened.

Three Errors

We have stated before that the basic error in this situation was the mingling of Law with grace. There are three grave errors that arise out of this. *First there is what we call "legalism."* This is the teaching that men are saved by works or human effort. That, in this case, would include the keeping of the Law and observing the rituals and ceremonies found in the Old Testament covenant God made with Israel. This same error is reflected today when someone claims to have done his best to keep the Ten Commandments. This to him is the way of salvation.

Paul makes very clear that anyone who is caught up in such an error has no foundation whatsoever for salvation. And this soul-condemning error is answered by Paul in the Book of Romans. Romans and Galatians are companion books on this whole area of truth. It is in Romans 3:28 that Paul writes, "Therefore we conclude that a man is justified by faith without the deeds of the law."

The second error that can undermine true faith in Jesus Christ is what we may call "false liberty." The Christian is called unto liberty, but that liberty is defined for us in the Scriptures and not left to our imagination. Yet there are those who teach that because they are saved by grace, it makes no difference how they live or behave. This Satanic error is answered in the Book of James. He wrote: "Even so faith, if it hath not works, is dead, being alone" (2:17). In other words, a faith that does not produce works is not real faith.

The third error is the one Paul deals with in his Letter to the Galatians. In fact, the error itself is often named "Galatianism." This false doctrine teaches that we are saved by grace but are kept saved by the Law. In reality this makes salvation dependent on our works. Our works of righteousness are to be a supplement to our faith for ultimate salvation. One must endure to the end by keeping the works of the Law if he is going to be saved. This is the error of Galatianism, the error that Paul combats in this brief Letter. Here we have the strongest arguments to be found in the Scriptures that we are saved and kept and ultimately redeemed from this world by the grace of God without the works of the Law. This teaching brings opposition from well-meaning people, but we must constantly refer to the Word of God for our information and truth in order to be safe.

Paul deals with this matter of persecution in chapter 4. He says according to verse 29: "But as then he that was born after the flesh persecuted him that was born after the Spirit, even so it is now." That is, those that are seeking to be saved on their own merit are going to be the enemies of those who are born of the Spirit of God and believe salvation is all of God. Yet the seriousness of bringing in works either to save us in the first place or to perfect our salvation is seen in the curse Paul pronounces on false teachers. Their teaching frustrates the grace of God and accuses God of needlessly sacrificing His Son, Jesus Christ. Galatianism is the subtlest of all errors concerning law-works in salvation.

CHAPTER TWO

CHRISTIAN LIBERTY

This Letter to the Galatians has been called the Magna Charta of the early Church. It is the declaration of the Christian's liberty in Christ. This is not a liberty to sin; this is liberty to please God without being bound under law, rules and regulations.

In writing to the Colossians on the same subject Paul declared: "If then you have died with Christ to material ways of looking at things and have escaped from the world's crude and elemental notions and teachings of externalism, why do you live as if you still belong to the world?—Why do you submit to rules and regulations? [such as], Do not handle [this], Do not taste [that], Do not even touch [them], Referring to things all of which perish with being used. To do this is to follow human precepts and doctrines. Such [practices] have indeed the outward appearance [that popularly passes] for wisdom, in promoting self-imposed rigor of devotion and delight in self-humiliation and severity of discipline of the body, but they are of no value in checking the indulgence of the flesh—the lower nature. [Instead, they do not honor God] but serve only to indulge the flesh" (Col. 2:20-23, Amp.).

What the Apostle is telling us here is that rules and regulations and laws do not check the flesh or the lower nature; instead they indulge it. The liberty in Christ sets us free to live for Christ in the power He supplies.

The Book of Galatians explains the nature of our liberty in Christ and shows us how to apply the principles of that liberty in our daily lives.

So essential is this to the Apostle that he, under the guidance of God, curses the enemy of that liberty. It is important that we see this, because this Epistle becomes a clarion call for the Church to return to freedom. This was Luther's letter. It found him when he was bound by a legalistic system and declared to him the true meaning of Christianity. He read in Galatians 3:11: "The just shall live by faith." That became his verse. And that is why he had such a great ministry in his day. He found the truth, acted upon it and proclaimed it.

Denunciation and Declaration

We cannot overlook the fact that this Letter is full of denunciations. These, however, must not be dealt with to the exclusion of the positive teaching. If we draw only on the negative, we will not get anywhere. A teaching that consists of do this and do that, or do not do this, does not help free the soul. We need not only the negative to point out what is wrong, but we must understand the positive teaching or we lose the message of the Book. We cannot really understand the force of the negative denunciations unless we are conscious of the truth which lies behind them. This is what we have to search out, this truth that God revealed to Paul. When we do, we will come to understand why he was so severe in his denunciations.

The teaching of the truth as it is in the Bible constitutes what we call the dynamic. It may cause divisions because it separates the false from the true. There is both the negative side and a positive side to truth. We must beware of the tendency to fight everybody and everything that goes wrong to the exclusion of declaring the positive gospel. Paul in the Galatian Letter proclaimed the truth of our liberty in Christ and protested and denounced everything that contradicted the truth of the Christian's liberty. But he kept these things in balance—denunciation and declaration. A key verse in this respect is Galatians 5:1: "Stand fast therefore in the liberty wherewith Christ hath made us free, and be not entangled again with the yoke of bondage." Our goal in this study is to see what liberty really is, how it operates, and how to keep from getting entangled in the yoke of bondage which will keep us from experiencing true Christian liberty.

This great truth of Christian liberty is expounded in the larger Epistle of Romans which we will have cause to refer to many times. In the Book of Galatians the great doctrine of Christian liberty is highlighted. This is done in three principal statements, and these have to do with three principal words.

Eternal Life

Paul first expounds the truth concerning life. He is speaking here of the Christian life and its only source. In the second place he takes up the subject of law, not rules and regulations of the Mosaic Covenant, but the law of Christ in us which is not a written law but a motivating power. The third subject is love which is the fruit of the Spirit. So then we have the three positive subjects dealt with in this Epistle, namely life, law and love.

In speaking of life we are speaking of eternal life, a particular kind of life. It is supplied by the Holy Spirit. It is not the turning over of a new leaf, or of trying new ways to live. It is Christ in us. It is not a mere principle. For example, during the Christmas season we often hear people speak of the "spirit of Christmas." By this they mean a particular kind of attitude toward life and toward others during that season of the year. But so far as the Christian is concerned Christmas is Christ. And eternal life is Christ. Our faith is in a Person who is our eternal life.

This is a God-produced life. Its source is the Holy Spirit. This is the argument of Paul in Galatians 3:3-5: "Are you so foolish and so senseless and so silly? Having begun [your new life spiritually] with the (Holy) Spirit, are you now reaching perfection [by dependence] on the flesh? . . . Then does He Who supplies you with His marvelous (Holy) Spirit, and works powerfully and miraculously among you, [do so on the grounds of your doing] what the Law demands, or because of your believing and adhering to and trusting in and relying on the message that you heard?" (Amp.). The Holy Spirit is the root of Christianity in us. God sent His Spirit to indwell us and the Spirit produces the resurrection life of Christ in us.

Paul deals with the same truth in Romans. He wrote: "But ye are not in the flesh, but in the Spirit, if so be that the Spirit of God dwell in you. Now if any man have not the Spirit of Christ, he is none of his. And if Christ be in you, the body is dead because of sin; but the Spirit is life because of righteousness" (Rom. 8:9,10). Here we will learn not only that the Spirit is in us but Christ is in us also. This is something we cannot explain because it involves the mystery of the Trinity—God the Father, God the Son and God the Holy Spirit. These are three distinct Persons, yet they are one. When one of the members of the Trinity indwells us, He not only represents the others but the others are present also. The Holy Spirit came to glorify Christ and He produces Christ in us.

The Apostle goes on to say in the following verse: "But if the Spirit of him that raised up Jesus from the dead dwell in you, he that raised up Christ from the dead shall also quicken your mortal bodies by his Spirit that dwelleth in you." This is life promised to us now, not in the future resurrection. This is a present form of the resurrection, a resurrection to life in our present experience. It is the manifestation of Christ in us the hope of our glory. Nothing but faith is needed for salvation. This is the emphatic teaching of Scripture.

To declare that works or law such as circumcision or baptism are necessary for salvation is to proclaim the most deadly heresy that can possibly be taught. How dare we be so bold in making this statement? For the simple reason that the Holy Spirit says it through Paul in the Book of Galatians: "If any man preach any other gospel . . . let him be accursed [anathema—doomed to perdition]" (Gal. 1:9). To add anything to faith for salvation is to destroy the very foundation of Christianity. Eternal life is given to an individual on the basis of faith only.

Law of Christ

In the second place the Christian is under a new law known as the "law of Christ:" "To them that are without law, [I am] without law, (being not without law to God, but unto the law to Christ)" (I Cor. 9:21). Included in this truth of the law of Christ is the fact that the Holy Spirit strives to form Christ in each believer. This Paul tells us in Galatians 4:19: "My little children, of whom I am again suffering birth pangs until Christ is completely and permanently formed (molded) within you" (Amp.).

The outworking of Christ's life which is in us is the result of our obedience to the desires of the Spirit. It is God who works in us both to will and to do of His good pleasure. This is why we are admonished to follow after the Spirit, and when we do, we will not fulfill the desires of the flesh.

We see from this, then, that the liberty we have in Christ is not a liberty to sin. There is no license to sin in the grace of God.

In John chapter 8 we have an incident which demonstrates this truth. Self-righteous scribes and Pharisees brought a woman to the Lord, a woman who had been caught in the act of sin. They said to Him that the Law would condemn such as she to be stoned to death, but they wanted to know what He said about it.

The Lord convicted all these men of sin, and they left. He turned to the woman and said to her: "Woman, where are those thine accusers? hath no man condemned thee? She said, No man, Lord. And Jesus said unto her, Neither do I condemn thee: go, and sin no more" (vv. 10,11). He did not say, "Go and live as you have been living and I'll forget it. Because the rest have not been able to accuse you I will not do so either." She had shown definitely that she believed Jesus Christ was her Saviour. The Lord said in so many words that He forgave her and would not condemn her; but now she must go and sin no more.

So this new life, this law of Christ which is a law of

liberty, is not a law to sin but a power to liberate us from the flesh nature which tries to keep us from doing right.

Freedom Through the Holy Spirit

Many of us because we are Christians try to do what is right, but we do not always accomplish it. Our trouble is that we have gone to the wrong place for our victory. Here is what Paul wrote: "For the law [principle] of the Spirit of life in Christ Jesus hath made me free from the law [principle] of sin and death" (Rom. 8:2). It is the Spirit of God who dwells in us who delivers us from the slavery of sin. When a man has life from the Holy Spirit by faith, he is set free from the bondage of the flesh.

Paul confessed in Romans 7: "I know that in me (that is, in my flesh,) dwelleth no good thing: for to will is present with me; but how to perform that which is good I find not. For the good that I would I do not: but the evil which I would not, that I do" (vv. 18,19). Such was the calamitous condition he found himself in, and in his desperation he cried out: "O wrteched man that I am! who shall deliver me from the body of this death?" (v. 24). Finally the truth dawned on him and he said, "I thank God through Jesus Christ our Lord" (v. 25). He found his deliverance was through Jesus Christ.

In Romans 8:13 Paul said, "For if we live after the flesh, ye shall die: but if ye through the Spirit do mortify the deeds of the body, ye shall live." We are unable in ourselves to put the works of the flesh in the place of death. Only the Holy Spirit makes this possible for us. Because we are Christians, we have the power that masters our flesh nature. God can do through us what He wants to do. By the Spirit of God the believer is made able to obey. This is true liberty— freedom to be able to obey God.

On the basis of Scripture we can make this even stronger statement: God makes us able not to sin. We are not saying here that a Christian does not sin, because all of us are conscious that we fall often. God, however, has provided for us all that is necessary to keep us from falling into sin. He has given us what is necessary to make it possible for us to obey Him.

No man is able to obey God just because he is circumcised, or has been baptized or because he follows rituals and ceremonies. Our obedience is due to the working of the Holy Spirit within us. Once we are born of God the Holy Spirit is there to stay and to work out God's desires in us. "For as many as are led by the Spirit of God, they are the sons of God" (Rom. 8:14). When the Spirit takes up His abode in us, He begins to lead us in paths that please God. In his Letter to the Philippians Paul wrote: "Wherefore, my beloved, as ye have always obeyed, not as in my presence only, but now much more in my absence, work out your own salvation with fear and trembling. For it is God which worketh in you both to will and to do of His good pleasure" (2:12,13). We can only work out our own salvation because that salvation is already in us. It is something God has given us and we are to allow it to work out through us.

Love

This leads us to the third subject, the subject of love. When we do what God wants us to do, the outworking of such a life will be expressed through love. Love is the fruit of the Spirit. It is the triumph of the Holy Spirit's work in our hearts.

In Galatians 5:22 we learn: "But the fruit of the Spirit is love." There are other virtues which follow, for also mentioned are joy, peace, longsuffering, gentleness, goodness, faith, meekness and temperance or self-control. Love, however, is basic. Love is the fulfilling of the Law. When God creates in us the fruit of love we will also have joy and peace and all the rest of the fruitage. Thus the whole life comes under the dominion of love.

In contrast to this the previous verses in Galatians 5 tell us of the works of the flesh. The Apostle does not speak of the fruit of the flesh but of its works. He lists a number of them and shows all of them to be evil, very wicked and vile.

Since this passage will be considered again, we will leave further discussion of it until later on in these studies.

Dead Ceremonies

When a man seeks to be righteous through ritualism, he evades God's righteousness. When we try to be good by following certain standards set up by men, even if these are religious standards, we will not accomplish the life of righteousness made possible only through the Holy Spirit. Instead of the righteousness of God in the life, we will open the door for the works of the flesh. If we follow these man-made standards of ritualism, we become self-satisfied; this produces pride, and pride opens the door for sins of various kinds creep in.

Religious systems have their rites and ceremonies and even creeds, but no life. Men, because they have fulfilled certain things that have been set up as standards, feel that this gives them license to do very much as they please after their religious exercises are over. Some seem to feel that going to church on Sunday gives them the right to do as they please any other time. A man once said to me: "I don't mix my religion with my business." This meant that so far as he was concerned he went to church on Sunday so that he could live as he wanted to the rest of the week. Ritualism does this for us, but it is not life. No wonder Paul said that any person preaching any other gospel than the true gospel of Christ was under the curse of God. A false gospel issues in the works of the flesh which are under the curse of God, for "they which do such things shall not inherit the kingdom of God" (Gal. 5:21). So the teachers of such false gospels are already under God's curse.

To trust in ceremonies for salvation from the guilt and consequences of sin is to deny Christ. To deny Christ is to be severed from Him and thus to be severed from eternal life. Such a person is under condemnation. So then, any ceremonies that men say are essential for salvation (note we are speaking of salvation), even baptism, come under the anathema of God. Baptism and the Lord's Supper, the assembling of ourselves for worship, are matters that follow once we are saved. But to make them necessary for salvation is to deny Christ, and to deny Christ is to be lost.

Are you going to heaven? If Jesus Christ should come today or tomorrow or the next day are you prepared to meet Him? Are you a born-again Christian? What is your gospel? Is it the true one? These are important things to consider. Our eternal destiny is at stake. It is well that we stop and evaluate our spiritual standing before God.

Some of the outward marks of Christianity are church attendance, Sunday school, prayer meeting and other activities associated with the church. But we may take part in all of these things and not be right with God. We need to evaluate our lives in the light of the Book of Galatians which has to do primarily with God's way of salvation and God's way to moral and spiritual maturity.

Salvation Only in Christ

We have already seen that salvation as well as Christian maturity lie altogether in Christ. Our behavior does not add anything to salvation itself or to progress in the Christian life. Our conduct may be proof that we are Christians and that we are growing, but our conduct is not the basis for these things.

Our salvation and our walk are basically matters of God's work in our behalf in answer to our faith.

We read in Romans 1:16,17: "For I am not ashamed of the gospel of Christ: for it is the power of God unto salvation to every one that believeth; "For therein is the righteousness of God revealed, from faith to faith: as it is written, The just shall live by faith."

Not only do we receive eternal life by faith, but we also live the Christian life by faith. This fact bears repetition. It is a truth that is taught throughout the Epistles of Paul. He wrote to the Colossians; "As ye have therefore received Christ Jesus the Lord, so walk ye in him" (2:6). How did we receive Christ? The answer of course is, by faith. So then we are to walk in Him by faith "rooted and built up in him, and established in faith, as ye have been taught, . . . Beware lest any man spoil you through philosophy and vain deceit, after the tradition of men, after the rudiments of the world, and not after Christ." This is a timely warning, for there is much philosophy today that is deceitful, leading us away from Christ. It stems from the traditions of men and is part of the rudiments of this world. We must center our attention and our faith in Christ: "For in him dwelleth all the fulness of the Godhead bodily" (2:9). Christ is sufficient for us. We are complete in Him.

All the blessings of God come to us through Christ. This was Paul's testimony in Romans 8:32 where he wrote: "He that spared not his own Son, but delivered him up for us all, how shall he not with him also freely give us all things?"

Looking again at what Paul wrote to the Colossians we read: "To whom God would make known what is the riches of the glories of this mystery among the Gentiles; which is Christ in you, the hope of glory: Whom we preach, warning every man, and teaching every man in all wisdom; that we may present every man perfect in Christ Jesus" (Col. 1:27-29). We find everything in Him or in union with Him. Because we are united to Him we have everything that God has for us.

If I am emphatic here concerning everything we have in Christ being ours on the basis of faith, it is because the Book of Galatians is emphatic on this very point. Whether it is salvation or Christian maturity, we receive it through trust in Christ. It is impossible without faith to please God according to Hebrews 11:6. And then Romans 14:23 tells us that "whatsoever is not of faith is sin." The emphasis on faith is found not only in the Book of Galatians but in all the Bible.

CHAPTER THREE

PAUL'S APOSTLESHIP AND MESSAGE

Three Divisions of Book

The first two chapters of Galatians are concerned with Paul's defense of his apostleship. The technique we see so often in our day of one person seeking to discredit another is nothing new in human affairs. It is employed a great deal in politics, but we also find it in Christian circles. Paul experienced it in his day. A group of false teachers came from Jerusalem to Galatia and told the Christians there that they had to observe the Law of Moses if they wanted to be saved. These Judaizers believed it was necessary for Christians to be circumcised and follow other points of the Law or they could not be saved. These teachers wanted the Galatians to become Jews before they could become Christians. But in order to make their teaching sound authoritative, the false teachers had to try to destroy Paul's character and authority as an apostle. Thus it was necessary for Paul to defend it, for his apostleship was tied in with his receiving the gospel and being commissioned to proclaim it.

Chapters 3 and 4 of Galatians are doctrinal. Here is where Paul explains what we have in the gospel and shows how it is superior to all religions. He shows us that justification is by faith alone apart from any mixture of works. He also emphasizes the superior authority of the gospel over Judaism and of the Holy Spirit over the flesh nature. We try so often by self-effort to be as God wants us to be and then find that we have failed. The apostle tells us that the Holy Spirit enables us to do what we could not do by ourselves. Paul also shows the superiority of faith over works. He does not exclude works when they are the result of faith, but he shows that faith is basic.

Paul reveals the superiority of being justified by faith over the condition of being in bondage to the Law. Some people claim they are keeping the Law, but in reality they are bound by that Law and cannot be justified by it.

Paul also shows us the superiority of being blessed over being cursed. He demonstrates the superiority of the promise in Abraham over the commands which came through Moses. He demonstrates the superiority of the Abrahamic Covenant over the Mosaic Covenant. He shows the superiority of Christian maturity over against what we might call child tutorage or the state of being a babe. The Apostle asserts the superiority of sonship over slavish bondsmanship. He makes clear the superiority of adoption or the setting forth of God's children as adult sons instead of being considered minors, and the superiority of liberty in Christ over the bondage of law and regulations.

Then in chapters 5 and 6 the Apostle shows how these great truths are very practical in their outworking in our daily lives. Some people think and say that the Christian life is hard to live, but Paul shows that that is due to them living under the bondage of self. The true gospel liberates us from regulations and creeds and makes it possible for us to live righteously and maturely before men and God.

He shows that true service springs from love instead of from law and bondage. The Law says you must do this or die. To a child we may say that he must do this or be spanked. But love does the work in the life of the Christian because the Holy Spirit is in us. So in this section also the Apostle emphasizes that the spiritual power in the believer through the Holy Spirit provides victory over the flesh.

Paul Defends His Apostleship

Instead of the usual salutation which is so often given in Paul's other letters, he begins Galatians in this way: "Paul, an apostle, (not of men, neither by man, but by Jesus Christ, and God the Father, who raised him from the dead)." Then he continues: "And all the brethren which are with me, unto the churches of Galatia: Grace be to you and peace from

God the Father, and from our Lord Jesus Christ, Who gave himself for our sins, that he might deliver us from this present evil world, according to the will of God and our Father: To whom be glory for ever and ever. Amen" (1:1-5).

Paul's reason for this abrupt introduction of his apostleship goes back to the fact that Judaizers who had come from Jerusalem sought to discredit the genuineness of his apostleship with the hope of thereby undermining the authenticity of his message.

It was because of the presence of Judaizers in the early Church that the great church council was held in Jerusalem. The record is in Acts 15 and there we learn: "And certain men which came down from Judea taught the brethren, and said, Except ye be circumcised after the manner of Moses, ye cannot be saved. . . . There rose up certain of the sect of the Pharisees which believed, saying, That it was needful to circumcise them, and to command them to keep the law of Moses" (vv. 1-5). So this kind of teaching had to be combatted in the early Church in various ways and in different places, but perhaps no place so vigorously as in the Galatian Church. Paul made it very plain that he was called to the apostleship not by any man or group of men but by Jesus Christ and God the Father, two members of the Divine Trinity. He said to the Romans: "I speak to you Gentiles, inasmuch as I am the apostle of the Gentiles, I magnify mine office" (Rom. 11:13). He asserted his position again in I Tim. 2:7 where he said: "Whereunto I am ordained a preacher, and an apostle, (I speak the truth in Christ, and lie not;) a teacher of the Gentiles in faith and verity."

How many apostles are named in the Bible? God recognized only twelve though we have at least thirteen mentioned. Is there a way of reconciling this difference?

In Revelation 21:14 we learn that the wall of the city "had twelve foundations, and in them the names of the twelve apostles of the Lamb." Paul writing to the Ephesians likened the Church to a temple with a superstructure built "upon the foundation of the apostles and prophets." So the foundation of the gospel was laid by the Apostles and then later on God said that as a result of it there will be twelve great stone foundations for the New Jerusalem with the names of the twelve Apostles on it. Our Lord mentioned twelve Apostles in Luke 22:29,30: "And I appoint unto you a kingdom, as my Father hath appointed unto me; That ye may eat and drink at my table in my kingdom, and sit on [twelve] thrones judging the twelve tribes of Israel."

Choosing an Apostle

Let us see where the problem lies. We turn to the first chapter of the Book of Acts where we find the Lord, in His last instructions to the Disciples before He ascended, commanded them that "they should not depart from Jerusalem, but wait for the promise of the Father, which, saith he, ye have heard of me" (Acts 1:4). The disciples waited in the neighborhood of 10 days and during that time we read of this event: "And in those days Peter stood up in the midst of the disciples, and said, (the number of names together were about an hundred and twenty,) Men and brethren, this scripture must needs have been fulfilled, which the Holy Ghost by the mouth of David spake before concerning Judas, which was guide to them that took Jesus. For he was numbered with us, and had obtained part of this ministry" (vv. 15-17). Then Peter went on to recount how Judas after betraying the Lord had hanged himself leaving his position vacant among the Disciples.

Here is what they did to remedy the lack in their number: "And they appointed two, Joseph called Barsabas, who was surnamed Justus, and Matthias. And they prayed, and said, Thou, Lord, which knowest the hearts of all men, shew whether of these two thou hast chosen, That he may take part of this ministry and apostleship, from which Judas by transgression fell, that he might go to his own place. And they gave forth their lots; and the lot fell upon Matthias; and he was numbered with the eleven apostles" (vv. 23-26). This appointing was done possibly by the eleven disciples and some of the others.

But we must remember that Jesus had told them to

wait until the Spirit came. When He came, He was to guide them and empower them and send them forth as witnesses. But they did not wait until the Spirit came to do something they thought should be done—putting someone in Judas' place.

This was done on the basis of standards the Disciples thought should be met, and they found two in their midst who met these standards. Then they asked God to choose between them.

I remember that some years ago I was on a board of a very fine Christian organization that had one rule I could not go along with. The rule was that 80 per cent of their number had to be of a certain denomination and the rest of them God could choose from other denominations. I could not go along with this position, believing that God should be given free choice of whomever He wanted and not for us to tell Him which ones to choose. But the Apostles chose two men and then asked God to choose between these men. They took lots and the lot fell on Matthias. Yet neither one of these men is ever mentioned again in the Bible. Personally I think that the impatient Peter had jumped the gun. Who gave him the power to ordain apostles?

As we study the passage in Galatians 1, we find that apostles were specially chosen individuals called and ordained of God. This we have already emphasized. Paul said he was not called of men, neither by men, but by Jesus Christ. Yet the disciples in the upper room limited God to two men and cast lots so, of course, one was bound to be chosen. God did not comment on this, neither did He punish them or judge them for it. He just did not recognize it.

When God chooses there is no question about the matter. We read in Acts 13:1: "As they ministered to the Lord, and fasted, the Holy Ghost said, Separate me Barnabas and Saul for the work whereunto I have called them." Here there could be no question as to who was called. Or as we read in I Timothy 2:7: "Whereunto I am ordained a preacher, and an apostle, (I speak the truth in Christ, and lie not)." Paul was ordained and chosen by Jesus Christ: "Paul, an apostle—special messenger appointed and commissioned and sent out—not from [any body of] men nor by or through any man, but by and through Jesus Christ, the Messiah, and God the Father Who raised Him from among the dead" (Gal. 1:1, Amp). Not men but God chose Paul.

Twelve times in the various Epistles Paul identified himself as an apostle chosen by Jesus Christ. Who chose the first twelve apostles? The Lord Jesus Himself did. Why did He choose Judas? This is something I cannot answer except to say that the Bible said He would and that God had a purpose in it. That one would betray our Lord was predicted and that another would take his place was to be expected. But this was to be all.

The Judaizers claimed that Paul was not an apostle because he was not chosen by them or ordained by the elders in the church at Jerusalem.

The way these things are said today is that so-and-so was not licensed by our group to preach. He has not been ordained by our ordination committee nor trained in our seminary.

Paul was not chosen by men but by the Lord Jesus Christ. Paul's particular ministry was to the Gentiles whereas Peter preached primarily to the Jews. They preached the same gospel, but they were chosen for different spheres of ministry. The Lord is the Lord of the harvest, and we should let Him do the choosing in this.

But why should we consider this matter at all? For the simple reason that Paul took two chapters in this Book to show his position and authority as an apostle of Jesus Christ. All Paul had he received from God, and so in the first two chapters in Galatians he vindicated his ministry, his method and his message.

The Gospel Stated

Paul stated what the gospel is in these words: "Who gave himself for our sins, that he might deliver us from this present evil world, according to the will of God and our Father" (Gal. 1:4). The gospel is simple and yet profound. This is the same gospel preached by all the apostles whether in Jerusalem or among the Gentiles. It is understandable that in preaching to Israelites, the apostles made some applications of a little different kind than they would to heathen Gentiles. After all, the two groups came from totally different social and religious backgrounds. But this did not mean a different gospel for each or a change in the gospel. It was the same gospel but applied in a way that was essential and understandable to whatever people were being evangelized. The presentation was the same in this regard that the gospel is in a Person, the Person of the Lord Jesus Christ, Himself. "For he that hath the Son hath life; and he that hath not the Son of God hath not life" (I John 5:12). "For other foundation can no man lay than that is laid, which is Jesus Christ" (I Cor. 3:11). "Neither is there salvation in any other; for there is none other name under heaven given among men, whereby we must be saved" (Acts 4:12).

Since we are living in the latter days of this age, days of religious confusion, it is necessary that we restate God's case concerning the gospel. We read in II Corinthians 5:21: "For he hath made him to be sin for us, who knew no sin; that we might be made the righteousness of God in him." God sees sin as a state of bondage from which man needs to be delivered. It is not a matter of our delivering ourselves by what we do but of being delivered and regenerated by God.

An illustration of this is found in the Old Testament. The people of Israel were in the land of Egypt and God said concerning them: "I have surely seen the affliction of my people which are in Egypt, and have heard their cry by reason of their taskmasters; for I know their sorrows; And I am come down to deliver them out of the hand of the Egyptians" (Ex. 3:7,8). They were in bondage; they were slaves; they could not free themselves. God had to do it for them.

The Scriptures teach us that we are bound by sin, and sin is abhorred by God. He sees us not only as sinful but as slaves to sin and also that we are dead in sin, utterly unable to help ourselves. This is brought out clearly in Ephesians 2:1-5: "And you hath he quickened, who were dead in trespasses and sins: Wherein in time past ye walked according to the course of this world, according to the prince of the power of the air, the spirit that now worketh in the children of disobedience: Among whom also we all had our conversation in times past in the lusts of our flesh, fulfilling the desires of the flesh and of the mind; and were by nature the children of wrath, even as others. [There is nothing we could do about it. We were slaves to sin.] But God, who is rich in mercy, for his great love wherewith he loved us, Even when we were dead in sins, hath quickened us together with Christ." What a wonderful, powerful gospel!

This same truth is given in a little different way in Colossians 1:12,13: "Giving thanks unto the Father, which hath made us meet to be partakers of the inheritance of the saints in light: Who hath delivered us from the power of darkness, and hath translated [transferred] us into the kingdom of his dear Son." He has taken us out of the kingdom of bondage and darkness and placed us into the kingdom of light, the kingdom of His Son. What a gospel! And it is in the Person of Jesus Christ.

The Lord Jesus Christ said, "And ye shall know the truth, and the truth shall make you free" (John 8:32). Some of His hearers refused to believe they were not free. They replied: "We be Abraham's seed and were never in bondage to any man; how sayest thou, Ye shall be made free?" (v. 33). "Jesus answered them, Verily, verily, I say unto you, Whosoever committeth sin is the servant of sin" (v. 34). That is radiantly clear. The person who sins is in bondage to sin. Then Jesus asserted: "If the Son therefore shall make you free, ye shall be free indeed" (v. 36). The Pharisees and scribes continued to argue the point, merely demonstrating their blindness due to their spiritual bondage.

Salvation is more than just rescuing us from the condemnation of sin. It includes deliverance or being made free from the slavery or bondage of sin in our daily experience; This is part of the significance of the following phrase in Galatians 1:4 in which the Saviour is declared to "deliver us from this present evil world." The Apostle also describes this as sanctifying or setting us apart from sin unto God.

The same truth is emphasized in Galatians 6:14 where Paul states: "But God forbid that I should glory, save in the cross of our Lord Jesus Christ, by whom the world is crucified unto me, and I unto the world." Not only did Christ die on the cross but we died with Him, and in that transaction we were crucified unto the world and the world to us. Thus through the cross we are separated from the power of the world that would seek to enslave us in sin.

The fact that Christ delivers us from this present evil world is inherent in the admonition given by Paul in Romans 12:1,2. We are admonished to yield our bodies to God and not to be "conformed to this world but to be transformed by the renewing of our minds." The word translated "transformed" is the same as is translated "transfigured" in connection with our Lord's experience on the Mount of Transfiguration. This is something supernatural. It is a change possible only because of the power of God. We are dead with Christ from the rudiments of the world according to Colossians 2:20, and the Lord makes available to us the power to be renewed as God wants us to be.

None of this is by human effort. It is all of grace. The gospel is a gospel of grace. Grace means that something was given to us that we did not deserve. God gives us new life in Christ because He loves us.

Only One Gospel

There has only been one gospel and God has offered it to man. This is evident in the study of the Scriptures from Genesis to Revelation. It may not always appear in the same words, but the same truth is there, nevertheless. The gospel has always been through God's Son Jesus Christ. This fact stands out in the very first message of the gospel. After man had sinned God made this statement to the serpent in the presence of Adam and Eve: "And I will put enmity between thee and the woman, and between thy seed and her seed; it shall bruise thy head, and thou shalt bruise his heel." The seed of the woman is Christ and this is the first promise of Christ's redemptive work in the Scriptures.

The next reference to it is an object lesson God gave Adam and Eve. We read in Genesis 3:21: "Unto Adam also and to his wife did the Lord God make coats of skins, and clothed them." This could not be done without the shedding of blood. In this case it was an innocent animal. The message was that God would provide a temporary covering for man's sins through the shedding of animals' blood until the time when His own Son would give His own blood for the sins of men.

The gospel as presented to Abraham was a gospel of salvation by faith and not of human effort. In Romans 4:3 we read: "For what saith the scripture? Abraham believed God, and it was counted unto him for righteousness." It was the same gospel as David understood it according to Psalm 51:7: "Purge me with hyssop, and I shall be clean: wash me, and I shall be whiter than snow." David knew that only God could cleanse and purify him. It had to be a work of God and not of man.

Isaiah believed and taught the same gospel. He said in speaking of Christ: "But he was wounded for our transgressions, he was bruised for our iniquities; the chastisement of our peace was upon him; and with his stripes we are healed" (53:5).

Jeremiah, another of the great prophets, knew only the same gospel. He said: "In his days Judah shall be saved, and Israel shall dwell safely: and this is his name whereby he shall be called, THE LORD OUR RIGHTEOUSNESS." The Lord is our righteousness, for we have none of our own. This is the testimony of Scripture.

John the Baptist preached the same gospel. He said of the Lord Jesus: "Behold the Lamb of God, which taketh away the sin of the world" (John 1:29).

Peter preached the same gospel also. He said according to Acts 4:12: "Neither is there salvation in any other: for there is none other name under heaven given among men, whereby we must be saved." Later on in Acts 10:43 Peter said, "To him [Christ] give all the prophets witness, that through his name whosoever believeth in him shall receive remission of sins."

John the beloved disciple says in his first letter: "But if we walk in the light, as he [Christ] is in the light, we have fellowship one with another, and the blood of Jesus Christ his Son cleanseth us from all sin" (I John 1:7).

There are some who say that these men preached only the gospel of the kingdom, but this evidence shows they all preached the gospel of the grace of God. There was a time when Jesus was on this earth living under the Law that He sent forth His disciples to preach the gospel of the coming kingdom. But it is clear from John's Gospel that the gospel of the grace of God was also taught. And certainly after Pentecost they all preached the same gospel.

Even James preached the gospel of the grace of God even though some may be inclined to think that he taught a gospel of works. He said, "With his own will begat he us with the word of truth, that we should be a kind of first fruits of his creatures" (Jas. 1:18). God begot us through His Word, the written Word opening our minds to the gospel and the Living Word, Christ, saving our souls.

Paul joined with all these others in the message he proclaimed. He said, "Be it known unto you therefore, men and brethren, that through this man [Jesus] is preached unto you the forgiveness of sins: And by him all that believe are justified from all things, from which ye could not be justified by the law of Moses" (Acts 13:38,39).

The last book in the Bible presents the same truth: "And from Jesus Christ, who is the faithful witness, and the first begotten of the dead, and the prince of the kings of the earth. Unto him that loved us, and washed us from our sins in his own blood" (Rev. 1:5). We are emphatic on this matter because the Bible is emphatic about it. This is serious. Human destiny is at stake. A Christian is one who trusts in the Lord Jesus Christ. Salvation is in a Person.

CHAPTER FOUR

WHAT IS A CHRISTIAN?

Look once again at Galatians 1:6,7 in the Amplified: "I am surprised and astonished that you are so quickly turning renegade and deserting Him Who invited and called you by the grace (unmerited favor) of Christ, the Messiah, [and that you are transferring your allegiance] to a different, even an opposition gospel. Not that there is [or could be] any other [genuine Gospel], but there are [obviously] some who are troubling and disturbing and bewildering you (with a different kind of teaching which they offer as a gospel) and want to prevert and distort the Gospel of Christ, the Messiah [into something which it absolutely is not]."

Human destiny is at stake here. We must have the correct answer to the question, what is and what is not a Christian? A grievous yet popular misconception of what a Christian really is, is everywhere present today. It is alarming that so many people hold to the error that the Christian life stems from a certain kind of conduct.

Do not misunderstand me. Good conduct results from a person being a Christian, but it is not the means of one becoming a Christian. The error lies in the belief that if we do certain things and do not do certain other things, we are Christians. Another group says we are to look to Christ as a Teacher or as the Way-shower to life. But this is to deal with life as a principle instead of recognizing the Person who is the Life. You may ask what the difference is. There is all the difference in the world! Following after a person does not make one a Christian. There is an old saying: "Going into the garage does not make you an automobile." Neither does going to church make one a Christian. It is not what we do that makes us Christians.

Others insist on adopting certain spiritual principles and thus acquiring a new set of habits. So the list is made for us: attend church; read the Bible and pray; have new associates; be fair in your dealings; follow the Golden Rule; take a Christain attitude toward certain questions of the day; conform to certain standards. Do all these and you will be a Christian, is what people try to tell us. This is Galatianism in its modern form.

What these people ignore is the inner change needed in a person that produces this kind of conduct. We have nothing against the conduct itself. But this conduct does not produce a Christain. There is something else needed to produce a Christian who then produces this conduct.

In Galatians Paul sets forth what the genuine distinguishing marks of a Christian really are. Any other so-called gospel puts a man automatically under the curse of God. I do not say this on my own authority. God said it here in the Book of Galatians. Eternal life is at stake. How can we be so careless as to project our own reasoning into these eternal issues!

The Bible says that all humanity is divided into one of the following two classes: "In Adam all die, even so in Christ shall all be made alive" (I Cor. 15:22). In other words, all who are the descendents of Adam die. All who are the descendents of Christ—and these are spiritual descendents, not physical ones—they shall live. According to the Scriptures we are sinners by birth. "Wherefore as by one man sin entered into the world, and death by sin; and so death passed upon all men, for that all have sinned" (Rom. 5:12). This is a fact. God said it. That settles it. It makes no difference what we think; our present reason, our higher knowledge or better learning does not change God's Word.

It is God who gives physical life to everybody. And it is also God who provides spiritual birth for those who trust in Christ. Through Adam they became members of the human race, and through faith in Christ they become members of the spiritual race in Christ. From Romans 5:18,19 we learn: "Therefore as by the offense of one judgment came upon all men to condemnation; even so by the righteousness of one [Jesus Christ] the free gift came upon all men unto justification of life. For as by one man's disobedience many were made sinners, so by the obedience of one shall many be made righteous."

Four Marks of a Christian

Now here are four marks of a Christian as set forth in the Book of Galatians. *First, a Christian is one who has the living Christ living in him.* "I am crucified with Christ: nevertheless I live; yet not I, but Christ liveth in me: and the life which I now live in the flesh I live by the faith of the Son of God, who loved me, and gave himself for me" (2:20). Or as we read in Galatians 4:19: "My little children, of whom I travail in birth again until Christ be formed in you." So a Christian is a person who has had a transforming experience through Christ. Have you had such an experience?

Second, a Christian is one who has the Holy Spirit within him, for in Galatians 4:6 we read: "And because ye are sons [if we are born again, if we are born of His family we are His sons], God sent forth the Spirit of His Son into your hearts." He is the One who really begets us or creates us anew and makes us believers. He also creates in us the new character from which Christian conduct comes. Christian conduct does not make a Christian, but a true Christian, one who is born of the Holy Spirit, will have Christian conduct as well. We learn from Galatians 5:22: "The fruit of the Spirit is love." We do not love in order to become Christians but we love because we are Christians. Then it is that love, joy, peace, longsuffering, gentleness, goodness, faith, meekness and temperance follow in the life. These are the fruit of Him who dwells in us.

In the third place, a Christian is one who has shared the cross experience with Christ as the basic solution of his personal problems. We all have come under this experience of the cross although we may not all have understood it.

The key text on this subject is as follows: "I am crucified with Christ: nevertheless I live; yet not I, but Christ liveth in me" (2:20). When Christ died, I died with Him and when He arose I arose with Him. We will see more of these truths at a later time, for they are vital to our spiritual health and welfare.

Galatians 5:24 says, "And they that are Christ's have crucified the flesh with the affections and lusts." This is a fact. Maybe we do not feel like it, or maybe we do not understand it, but it is something that has already taken place. Galatians 6:14 says, "But God forbid that I should glory, save in the cross of our Lord Jesus Christ, by whom the world is crucified unto me, and I unto the world." No wonder Paul says in 6:17: "From henceforth let no man trouble me: for I bear in my body the marks of the Lord Jesus Christ."

In the fourth place, the Christian is one who is possessed of a life that is so divine, so ideal, that it cannot be pushed into a mold of external regulations. We have a new life, a life from God which is Christ Himself. We cannot take this life and put it under the domination of rules and regulations. It is true that God gives us many things to look at in order to see what we should be like if we are born-again Christians. If we do not measure up, there is something wrong.

Let us look at Galatians 4:9-11: "But now, after that ye have known God, or rather are known of God, how turn ye again to the weak and beggarly elements, whereunto ye desire again to be in bondage? Ye observe days, and months, and times, and years. I am afraid of you, lest I have bestowed upon you labour in vain." Then: "My little children, of whom I travail in birth again until Christ be formed in you, I desire to be present with you now, and to change my voice; for I stand in doubt of you. Tell me, ye that desire to be under the law, do ye not hear the law?" (4:19-21). Do we not hear what the Law has to say and how it will condemn us? That is all it can do—condemn us. We may say, "Well, we are trying to live by it," but it will not save us. All it can do is condemn us because we cannot live by it.

Perhaps we ask then if we should be lawless in our conduct. Indeed not. We are under a new law. It is Christ in us and He is our new life. Galatians 5:1 says, "Stand fast therefore in the liberty wherewith Christ has made us free, and be not entangled again with the yoke of bondage." The Christian, as we have repeatedly pointed out, is one who is possessed with new life, the life of Jesus Christ Himself. We are partakers of His nature. We cannot be subjected to all the laws, rules, and regulations of this kind again and condemned by them because we are freed by Him. We are not free to sin but free to let Him live out His life in us.

The Apostle continues in 5:2: "Behold, I Paul say unto you, that if ye be circumcised, Christ shall profit you nothing. But I testify again to every man that is circumcised, that he is a debtor to do the whole law. Christ is become of no effect unto you, whosoever of you are justified by the law; ye are fallen from grace. For in Jesus Christ neither circumcision availeth any thing, nor uncircumcision; but faith which worketh by love" (vv. 2-6). In other words, the Christian life consists not first of behavior but of being, the behavior coming out of the being. It is a kind of being out of which righteous behavior naturally proceeds. Do not put the cart before the horse. It is not first something external but something internal. It is the root which produces the fruit. All life is this way. Corn produces more corn because it is corn. Wheat produces more wheat because it is wheat.

The Christian life must be free to express itself and not be held down by man-made regulations and resolutions, Thus it will express itself correctly. If it does not express itself in the right way, it is not the new life. It is impossible for Christ to come in and make His life in us or be the life in us without Him expressing His life. If He does not come in, there is no expression of the Christ life. And if He is not present, we are not born of God. Have you received Jesus Christ as your life?

Grace and Law Exclude Each Other

The Lord Jesus made a startling statement when He said, "He that is not with me is against me." He made it clear that there is no middle ground with regard to Him. The only right side to be on is His side.

Moses, speaking for the Lord, said to the people of Israel, "I have set before you life and death . . . therefore choose life" (Deut. 30:19). This is still the choice before men and the choice before us. We can choose God's way and find life, or we can reject it and find death.

This was what so concerned Paul when he wrote to the Galatians. He was deeply alarmed that they were so soon removed from Christ. God had called them to find life in Christ and was working in their lives to perfect the work begun there. Yet the Galatian Christians had turned from the true gospel, and in turning from it they had removed themselves from the Person of Christ.

They did this by mixing law and grace. God calls men and women into the grace of Christ. The gospel begins with God. Salvation is from Him. We were in no position to help ourselves "But God, who is rich in mercy, for his great love wherewith he loved us, Even when we were dead in sins, hath quickened us together with Christ" (Eph. 2:4,5).

This is all based on the grace of God. It is a gift from God and not at all according to what we deserve. We do not merit salvation. God provides it for us because He loves us; and when we receive Christ as personal Saviour, God gives us salvation. Parents with children will understand this. We often give our children things that perhaps they do not deserve, but we give these things because we love them. Salvation is by grace through faith as the Apostle says in Ephesians 2:8,9: "For by grace are ye saved through faith; and that not of yourselves: it is the gift of God: Not of works, lest any man should boast."

Grace and works are the opposite of each other. They exclude each other. Salvation cannot be partly by grace and partly by works. It must be either all of the one or all of the other. This is the teaching of Romans 11:6: "And if by grace, then is it no more of works: otherwise grace is no more grace. But if it be of works, then is it no more grace: otherwise work is no more work."

The distinction is maintained in another portion of Romans: "Now to him that worketh is the reward not reckoned of grace, but of debt" (4:4). Wages received for work done is not a gift but the due reward of labor. Men receive wages because they have earned them, but God does not save us this way. The record continues: "But to him that worketh not, but believeth on him that justifieth the ungodly, his faith is counted for righteousness." There is no other way for us to be saved than by the grace of God which provides salvation as a gift.

Now grace becomes a test of the gospel. "If the message excludes grace, or mingles law with grace as the means either of justification or sanctification" it denies God's Word and makes salvation impossible to men.

The gospel does not start with us but with God. It is because God loves us and provides salvation through grace for us that we can be saved. And all of this centers in the Person of Jesus Christ. Salvation is consummated through Him. Moreover, salvation includes union with Him which in itself is a concept that goes beyond any imagination of man. We read in Ephesians 2:10: "For we are his workmanship created in Christ Jesus unto good works." This tells us that God has spiritually recreated us and placed us into union with Christ. Christ is in us as our life.

The same truth is taught by Paul in Galatians 2:20 where he says, "For I am crucified with Christ: nevertheless I live; yet not I, but Christ liveth in me." Or as the Apostle tells us in Colossians 1:27: "Christ in you, the hope of glory." John the Apostle testifies to the same truth when he says, "He that hath the Son hath life; and he that hath not the Son of God hath not life" (I John 5:12). Or as the same Apostle wrote in the Gospel of John: "As many as received him, to them gave he power to become the sons of God, even to them that believe on his name: Which were born, not of blood, nor of the will of the flesh, nor of the will of man, but of God" (John 1:12,13).

Under a Curse

So then, the gospel originates with God. It is by grace, and grace excludes the possibility of works for producing this salvation. It is consummated through God's Son Jesus Christ. Is it any wonder, then, that Paul was alarmed and distressed at the removal of the Galatian believers from Christ? They embraced another gospel which Paul said was not another. We have already seen what he meant. Two words are used in the original language and translated "another." The so-called gospel taught by the Judaizers and embraced by the Galatians was not a gospel the same as Paul had brought them, but a gospel of another kind. A so-called gospel that mixed the law and grace was not good but evil. There is but one true gospel, and any imitation or counterfeit has the anathema or curse of God upon it.

This curse does not come upon such a person at some later time but already rests on the person who mixes law and grace. This is what the Apostle tells us: "For as many as are of the works of the law are under the curse: for it is written, Cursed is every one that continueth not in all the things which are written in the book of the law to do them." Now it is very clear that no man is able of himself to do all the things that the Law requires. Consequently, the Law condemns him. Such a person is under God's anathema.

God Himself safeguards His gospel. He has marked it out very clearly so that we need not go astray with regard to it. The person who mixes law and grace is already under the anathema of God and can only be removed from that position as he turns to Christ: "Christ has redeemed us from the curse of the law, being made a curse for us: for it is written, Cursed is every one that hangeth on a tree" (Gal. 3:13). There is no other way for the curse of God to be removed from a person's life than for that one to believe in Christ.

While the true gospel and the false gospel may on the surface look to be the same, they are actually diametrically opposed to each other. To one not wholly familiar with American currency a counterfeit note may look like a good one, but a person trained to know the true from the false would have little trouble spotting the counterfeit. Christians must become experts in the knowledge of the gospel so that they themselves will not be deceived. They will be in a position to help deliver others who have been trapped by Satan's imitation.

Our Saviour warned of the program of Satan to deceive. In one of His parables He said, "The kingdom of heaven is likened unto a man which sowed good seed in his field: But while men slept, his enemy came and sowed tares among the wheat, and went his way. But when the blade was sprung up, and brought forth fruit, then appeared the tares also" (Matt. 13:24-26). In the early stage of growth the tares are hard to distinguish from the wheat. This is part of Satan's strategy and we must be alert to it.

CHAPTER FIVE

CHRIST AND THE BIBLE ARE UNIQUE

Up to now we have been considering somewhat the false gospel, but we need to know clearly what the true gospel is. It is necessary to expose the false and this some might term the negative approach; but it is essential that the positive aspect be expressed. We need to know beyond the shadow of a doubt what the true gospel is. We have seen that a false gospel mixes law and grace. It combines human works and effort with the work of God. This, in reality, cancels out God's work.

We have also seen that the true gospel centers or is consummated in the supernatural Person, Jesus Christ. It is no wonder then that Paul wrote: "I am not ashamed of the gospel of Christ: for it is the power of God unto salvation to every one that believeth" (Rom. 1:16). There is only one Christ of history and prophecy. The record is given to us with many unchangeable facts concerning Him. No one else could possibly fit His description. He is unique. There is not another like Him.

Seven Unalterable Facts About Christ

First of all, Jesus Christ had a supernatural birth. Reference to this is made very clearly in Galatians 4:4: "But when the fulness of the time was come, God sent forth his Son, made of a woman, made under the law."

The expression "made of a woman" is unusual. What is signified by this? The answer is found in Genesis 3:15 where the first great promise of the gospel is given. Here the coming of Christ is promised as "the seed of the woman." And the reason this language is used is that He was to be born miraculously.

49

The Lord Jesus Christ always existed, but in order that He might die for the sins of men, He had to become man. To become man He could not take upon Himself sinful human nature. A child born of a man and woman is born with the fallen nature. Our Lord was born of a virgin, conceived in her by the Holy Spirit. He had no human father. He was born without sin.

He was virgin-born according to the Scriptures. To deny this is to deny an essential uniqueness clearly emphasized by the Scriptures. God saw to it that the body in which Jesus Christ lived was prepared for Him by a woman; though she was not sinless, sin was not transmitted through her to Him. He was that "holy thing" who was born of Mary. This is an essential factor in the gospel.

In the second place, He had a kind of teaching which was unique. We read in Luke 4:22: "And all bare him witness, and wondered at the gracious words which proceeded out of his mouth. And they said, Is not this Joseph's son?" They could not understand how such wonderful teaching could come from a man who had not received formal education in the universities of that day.

The same testimony is given in John 7:46. It was said of Christ: "Never a man spake like this man." In all the learning of the 1900 and more years since Christ was here, nothing of His teaching has been outmoded. It is still as vital and up to date now as it was then. Present-day textbooks used in our schools are antiquated in just a few years. Man is ever learning, but the teaching our Lord gave never needed to be changed. It stands today and will stand for all eternity.

In the third place, Christ never needed to apologize for anything He did. What He did was perfect, without need of moral correction. In speaking to the scribes and Pharisees He asked them, "Which of you convinceth me of sin?" (John 8:46). Not one could point a finger at Him. When He stood on trial before Pilate accused of being a lawbreaker, Pilate said of Him, "I find no fault in this man" (Luke 23:4). Again in verse 14 we read Pilate saying, "Ye have brought this man unto me, as one that perverteth the people: and, behold, I, having examined him before you, have found no fault in this man touching those things whereof ye accuse him."

Our Lord's testimony to the Law bears out this fact. He said, "Think not that I am come to destroy the law, or the prophets: I am not come to destroy, but to fulfil. For verily I say unto you, Till heaven and earth pass, one jot or one tittle shall in no wise pass from the law, till all be fulfilled" (Matt. 5:17,18). He did not come to break the Law but to fulfill it. He alone of all men was able to do this.

We learn in Galatians 3:19 that the Law was added because of transgressions till the seed should come. The Law was given to show man that he was a sinful being and to awaken him to his need of salvation. Only our Lord kept the Law perfectly thus proving Himself to be sinless. At the same time He bore the curse of the broken Law by dying for us. Thus He fulfilled the Law. In what respect the Law has been set aside will be a subject for future consideration in these studies. The point here is that Christ had a unique life, then that He was sinless. No one but a sinless being could provide salvation for men.

In the fourth place, Christ had a supernatural death. He was the one man who had no need to die. Death is the result of sin, for "the wages of sin is death." He committed no sin and there was no sin in Him, and yet He came to die for our sins.

He purposely set about to give His life for us. We read in John 12:27: "Now is my soul troubled; and what shall I say? Father, save me from this hour: but for this cause came I unto this hour." A little later He said, "And I, if I be lifted up from the earth, will draw all men unto me. This he said, signifying what death he should die" (John 12:32,33). His death, then, was unique in that He did not have to die for Himself.

Furthermore His death was unique and supernatural in that no one could take His life. For Him to die He had to give it up. He said according to John 10:17: "Therefore doth my Father love me, because I lay down my life, that I might take it again. No man taketh it from me." He had power, He said, to lay it down and He had power to take it again. This was something He received from His Father. He was one Person who came into this world for the purpose of dying.

The uniqueness of that death is seen in the way He died. The centurion in charge of the crucifixion had undoubtedly seen many men die, but Christ's death was unique. The soldier witnessed the remarkable things that took place while Christ was on the cross and heard the things that He said and the final words He spoke, then said, "Certainly this was a righteous man" (Luke 23:47). And joining with some other witnesses the centurion said also: "Truly this was the Son of God" (Matt. 27:54).

Christ accomplished His life work by His death. This is the plain teaching of Hebrews 2:14: "He also himself likewise took part of the same [flesh and blood]; that through death he might destroy him that had the power of death, that is, the devil; And deliver them who through fear of death were all their lifetime subject to bondage." There is no question then but that Christ had a unique and supernatural death.

In the fifth place, He had a supernatural resurrection. The cemetery somehow has a way of holding those bodies committed to it. But Jesus had predicted that He would rise again from the grave, and He did.

According to Romans 1:4 our Lord "was declared to be the Son of God with power, according to the spirit of holiness, by the resurrection from the dead." His resurrection is often denied these days, but the facts concerning it cannot be set aside. The testimony of Acts 1:3 is, "He showed himself alive after his passion by many infallible proofs, being seen of them forty days, and speaking of the things pertaining to the kingdom of God." The 15th chapter of I Corinthians gives in detail how many people actually saw our Lord after His resurrection. Though some of the so-called learned men of our day do not want to believe in the miracle of the resurrection, they cannot erase the facts of it from the historical record.

In the sixth place, Christ has a unique heavenly ministry.

This is a comforting and encouraging truth. We read in Hebrews 9:24: "For Christ is not entered into the holy places made with hands, which are the figures of the true; but into heaven itself, now to appear in the presence of God for us." He is our heavenly and holy Attorney appearing on our behalf. He is able to save us to the uttermost seeing He ever lives to make intercession for us (Heb. 7:25). John comments on this fact when he writes: "These things write I unto you, that ye sin not. And if any man sin, we have an advocate with the Father, Jesus Christ the righteous" (I John 2:1).

He is both our Advocate and High Priest in the heavenlies, appearing before God for us. His is, indeed, a unique heavenly ministry.

In the seventh place, and this is our final consideration, *Christ will have a supernatural return.* This return will climax His ministry. He comforted the disciples by telling them, "Let not your heart be troubled: ye believe in God, believe also in me. In my Father's house are many mansions: if it were not so, I would have told you. I go to prepare a place for you. And if I go and prepare a place for you, I will come again, and receive you unto myself; that where I am, there ye may be also" (John 14:1-3).

He will come for His own and He will reward them when He comes. This is the teaching of Matthew 16:27: "For the Son of man shall come in the glory of his Father with his angels; and then he shall reward every man according to his works."

A Supernatural Book

These are unalterable facts of history and this final one of prophecy. They cannot be removed from the record. And all of them have been given through a supernatural Book, the Book which is the revelation of God to man.

The source and purpose of this Book are stated for us in II Timothy 3:16,17: "All scripture is given by inspiration of God, and is profitable for doctrine, for reproof, for correction, for instruction in righteousness: That the man of God may be perfect, throughly furnished unto all good works."

The expression "thus saith the Lord" is found some 361 times in the Bible. God gave this Book to us through the inspiration of the Holy Spirit and in it tells who Christ is and why He came. Shortly after His resurrection, our Saviour walked to Emmaus with two of His disciples and disclosed to them what is in the Word. "And beginning at Moses and all the prophets, he expounded unto them in all the scriptures the things concerning himself" (Luke 24:27). He showed that the Scriptures taught about Him. They explained His coming and what His death and resurrection signified. These facts were all laid out beforehand in the Old Testament. In Luke 24:44 our Saviour said, "These are the words which I spake unto you, while I was yet with you, that all things must be fulfilled, which were written in the law of Moses, and in the prophets, and in the psalms, concerning me."

The Lord did not leave the gospel facts to be interpreted by our own natural abilities. He has put His own authoritative interpretation on these facts so that we have no excuse if we misunderstand why Christ died and rose again.

In writing to the Corinthians Paul listed the essential facts of the gospel and showed that what Christ did in living and dying and rising again from the dead was according to the Scriptures. It is in the Scriptures we learn that Christ's death was not an ordinary death, as we have already seen. Some might say that all of us die but that does not tell us why Christ died. The Bible, however, tells us that He died for our sins. This is God's evaluation of Christ's death. All of these events were according to God's determined plan and purpose.

It is well for us to remember that these great truths were given before Christ came as well as being dealt with after He came and returned to glory. For example, Isaiah says: "But he was wounded for our transgressions, he was bruised for our iniquities: the chastisement of our peace was upon him; and with his stripes we are healed. All we like sheep have gone astray; we have turned every one to his own way; and the Lord hath laid on him the iniquity of us all" (53:5,6). We cannot emphasize too much the fact that this is

God's interpretation of Christ's work on Calvary, His death on our behalf. No matter what men may think, this is what God says and this is what counts. We will be judged by what God has said concerning His Son, not by what we want to think about it.

Paul wrote in Romans 4:25: "Who was delivered for our offences, and was raised again for our justification." Many would like to tell us that Jesus died merely as a martyr, or as an example, but the Scriptures make it very plain that Christ died as our substitute. And how clearly Isaiah saw this: "Yet it pleased the Lord to bruise him; he hath put him to grief: when thou shalt make his soul an offering for sin, he shall see his seed, he shall prolong his days, and the pleasure of the Lord shall prosper in his hand" (53:10). A parallel passage to this in the New Testament is II Corinthians 5:21: "For he hath made him to be sin for us, who knew no sin; that we might be made the righteousness of God in him." The fact is evident: the gospel can only be explained through a supernatural Book, the Word of God itself.

A Supernatural Experience

God the Son came to offer Himself as a sacrifice in order to deliver us. We have already seen how this is explained for us in the Scriptures. More, however, is needed. There must be a personal experience of these things in our own lives. This is the work of the Holy Spirit who gives us the experience which is regeneration or the new birth. We are saved by grace without works according to Ephesians 2:8,9. Then in verse 10 we are told we are God's workmanship created in Christ Jesus unto good works which God had before ordained that we should walk in them. Though the word "in" is a very small word in our language, it is one of the most important words in all of Scripture. Sometimes it merely speaks of location, but in this passage it speaks of union. Through the operation of the Holy Spirit we are united to Christ. We are one with Him. This is one of the great factors of salvation which turning over a new leaf could never bring about.

Paul had such an experience. He tells about it in Galatians 1:15,16: "But when it pleased God, who separated me from my mother's womb, and called me by his grace, To reveal his Son in me, that I might preach him among the heathen; immediately I conferred not with flesh and blood." Christ made a new creature out of him, became his life, and gave him the responsibility of preaching the gospel to the heathen. This was why Paul could say, "I am crucified with Christ: nevertheless I live; yet not I, but Christ liveth in me: and the life which I now live in the flesh I live by the faith of the Son of God, who loved me, and gave himself for me" (Gal. 2:20).

It is well to be reminded again of Galatians 4:19 which teaches very much the same truth: "My little children, of whom I travail in birth again until Christ be formed in you." This speaks of a supernatural experience, one that is possible only through the operation of the Holy Spirit. When Christ came the first time to this earth, there was a body prepared for Him and He lived in it. He was crucified and His body laid in the grave, and then He was resurrected. Today He is in the heavenlies in His glorified body; and yet, remarkable as it is, He lives in us. Through the Holy Spirit He lives in your body and my body. When the Holy Spirit unites us to Christ, we enter into an experience that reproduces the life of Christ in us.

Identification With Christ

We died with Him, for this is the testimony of Scriptures "I am crucified with Christ" is what Paul has already told us. Or, as he says in Colossians 2:20, we have died with Christ. Farther on in the Colossian Letter he states emphatically that we died, and our life is hid with Christ in God (3:3).

Not only did we die with Christ but we also arose with Him when He arose from the dead. In a spiritual sense, then, we are raised with Him and have received new life. "If ye then be risen with Christ" is what Paul states in Colossians 3:1 as a fact of salvation. There is no question about it. It is an established fact. In Ephesians 2:5,6 we are told: "Even when we were dead in sins, hath quickened us together with Christ, . . . And hath raised us up together, and made us sit together in heavenly places in Christ Jesus." So we are new creatures in Christ Jesus, raised from the dead—all by faith.

In the third place, Christ has appeared in heaven. We learn from Scripture that this is our experience also. We are dead and our life is hid with Christ in God. We are united to Christ and our life is hidden in Him. So closely are we united to our Saviour that we are told: "When Christ, who is our life, shall appear, then shall ye also appear with him in glory" (Col. 3:4). All of this is due to the Holy Spirit indwelling us and forming Christ in us. The Spirit reproduces the very character of Christ in our lives. This is evidenced by the fruit of the Spirit which is love, joy, peace, and many other spiritual graces.

We are made spiritually complete because of our union with Christ. Paul wrote to the Colossians: "For in him dwelleth all the fulness of the Godhead bodily. And ye are complete in him, which is the head of all principality and power" (2:9,10). Christlikeness is absolutely unobtainable save only as Christ lives in us. Only the Holy Spirit can reproduce the life of Christ in us. This is essential in the matter of salvation. Unless His life is in us and reproduced in us we are not saved.

This is the higher reaching down to the lower, a situation we find in science. The lower cannot reach up to the higher but the higher can reach down to the lower. The Lord is the highest of all, and He reaches down to human life to exalt us. It is not possible for us to reach up into the sphere of life where God lives and become part of it. But God can lift us up there, providing us with a new life in Christ.

I heard someone ask this question: "Did God create man or did man create God?" Some may think this is an absurd question, but there is reason for asking it since there are people today who believe that man did create God.

Now, the Bible teaches that in the beginning God created the heaven and the earth. Later He created man. Not all men, however, want to be subject to the Bible and its teaching. They realize they need something, however, so present-day men in their unbelief have invented a god for themselves. They have created a god of their own thinking that they can reach up to. But this is not reality. This is man's unbelieving imagination at work. The Bible teaches something entirely different.

God has taken into account man's need and man's heart of unbelief and has provided a salvation that meets man's basic need. Man's way is an impossible way. God's way is this: "For by grace are ye saved through faith; and that not of yourselves: it is the gift of God: Not of works, lest any man should boast. For we are his workmanship, created in Christ Jesus" (Eph. 2:8-10).

The heart of the natural man is in such rebellion against God that it is no wonder false teachers came to the Galatian churches with an imitation gospel. These teachers troubled the believers by trying to get them to accept a system of law keeping in place of the pure grace of God for salvation. By their meaningless religious talk and quoting of Scripture out of context, the false teachers deceived the people and discredited the gospel. And of course, they also discredited the messenger whom God had sent to Galatia with the gospel.

These tactics though old are practiced today. There are those who tell us that we need to add the Law to the grace of God. They want human works added to God's work. They say that anyone who preaches the gospel of pure grace is preaching an incomplete gospel. They heap scorn on the learning of the person who believes the Scriptures and speaks of them as out-of-date and sticking by old stuff that is shopworn and should be discarded.

Zealous But Wrong

Paul warned of the false teachers in his day when he said, "These men [the Judaizing teachers] are zealously trying to dazzle you—paying court to you, making much of you; but the purpose is not honorable or worthy or for any good. What they want to do is to isolate you [from us who oppose them], so that they may win you over to their side and get you to court their favor" (Gal. 4:17, Amp.). With a show of flattery and zeal the Judaizers tried to win over these Christians who for a time were impressed.

Because a person has much zeal does not mean he has the truth. What a person teaches must agree with the Holy Scriptures if the teaching is to be right. Zeal in itself is anything but sufficient. Paul commented in Galatians 4:18: "It is always a fine thing [of course] to be zealously sought after [as you are, provided that it is] for a good purpose and done by reason of purity of heart and life, and not just when I am present with you!" (Amp.).

The Judaizers perverted the gospel of Jesus Christ. That is, they twisted or distorted it. They apparently did not deny grace entirely, but they added law works to it. Such a gospel does not save anyone. And we might well ask ourselves if we are saved by God's grace, nothing added, or if we are just hanging on. If that is our condition, we can be sure that we will not hang on very long. Unless He holds us, salvation is impossible to us.

Proud Man

The real problem today just as it was in Paul's day, lies in the nature of man himself. Man is proud. He is especially proud of his own thinking. He wants freedom to think his own thoughts and not be bound by a revelation from God. This is what we see everywhere today. Man does not want to be controlled by what God says. It leaves him no room for speculation or human reasoning. He likes to discover what he calls truth and then claims it as his own.

The first two boys born into this world ran into the same problem. Cain decided he did not like God's way and tried to set up his own way of getting right with God. But he did not get any place.

Paul exhorted Timothy and all who belonged to the Lord to "preach the Word." But man would rather have his own thinking and preach his own ideas. They even twist the Bible to suit their own ways of thinking. They preach the ethical teachings of Jesus and ignore the theology of Paul.

The Lord Jesus promised that the Holy Spirit would come and lead believers into all truth. Part of that truth was given through Paul. Men today do not want what Paul taught because it does not jibe with their thinking. They want to put their own interpretation on what our Lord taught. But in doing this, they exclude any supernatural element in Christ's teaching such as His miracles and His deity. They feel quite free to speculate on what Christ's teaching really meant and how how it can be applied in such a way as to please the modern mind.

We must study and follow the teachings of Christ, for they are foundational. But their meaning does not always come clear to us until we study the Epistles where the great foundation facts of truth are interpreted for us by men God appointed for this great work.

Needed today is a renewed fear among men of God's anathema. We need to get back to the Bible God gave us and to the Christ of the whole Bible. Paul, in contrast to the false teachers, disclaimed any desire of trying to please men (Gal. 1:10). He wanted to please God, for he was the servant of Christ. Paul was not a man pleaser. He knew God's will and wanted to do it. The same could be said of Paul as was said of David in the Old Testament. God raised up David to be the king of Israel because He found in David a man after His own heart who would fulfill all His will. This was true of Paul also. His one great desire in life was to do the will of God.

Paul warned that in the last days "the time will come when they will not endure sound doctrine; but after their own lusts shall they heap themselves teachers, having itching ears; And they shall turn away their ears from the truth, and shall be turned unto fables" (II Tim. 4:3,4). But so far as Paul was concerned, he was ready to be offered. The time of his departure was at hand. While he lived for the Lord he was faithful. He fought a good fight and finished his course. He kept the faith.

The only way we can keep a faithful witness before men is to do as Paul exhorted Timothy to do. The Apostle charged him before God and the Lord Jesus Christ who will judge the quick and the dead at His appearing and kingdom, to preach the Word and to be instant in season and out of season, reproving, rebuking and exhorting with all longsuffering and doctrine. We must give men the whole Bible. The Epistles interpret for us what Jesus' words meant and what God's purposes are. All the Bible is inspired of God, not just part of it.

CHAPTER SIX

THE GOSPEL FROM GOD CHANGED PAUL

The Apostle Paul was himself a clear illustration of what the gospel can do in a life. If ever a man demonstrated the change Christ brings, Paul was that man. A life-changing event thoroughly transformed him in character and purpose.

Paul tells us in Galatians how he received the gospel and where it came from. He declared in Galatians 1:11: "For I want you to know, brethren, that the Gospel which was proclaimed and made known by me is not man's gospel—a human invention, according to or patterned after any human standard" (Amp.). Paul did not preach his own ideas, nor did he get his ideas from great teachers or men of vast learning. The gospel he proclaimed was not a human invention at all, for men do not think in terms of grace but of human effort.

Many people today are quite satisfied with their religious condition because they believe in God; they believe with sincerity and consider such belief is all that is necessary. The heart of the natural man does not even come close to devising such a gospel as is presented in the Bible. Some religions set forth ethical and moral ideals and require or encourage men to meet them. Yet these religions do not meet man at the point of his greatest need. Theirs is a system of works that allows a man to pat himself on the back and be proud of his accomplishments.

The gospel of Christ, on the other hand, tells of a work already done and makes it very clear that there is nothing man can do to improve what God has done through Christ. The natural man does not like this, for it does not cater to his pride; rather, it humbles him. No, Paul did not get his gospel from any man.

Paul said the gospel came to him as a direct revelation

from Christ: "For indeed I did not receive it from man, nor was I taught it; [it came to me] through a [direct] revelation [given] by Jesus Christ, the Messiah" (1:12, Amp.). Neither the original gift of the gospel to Paul nor the detailed meaning of it came to him from any man. The Apostle did not sit down and try to reason it out. God gave it to him line upon line, and that is what he preached.

There is no book in the world which is more misinterpreted than the Bible. People will take a verse out of its context and read into it their own interpretation. Some talk about the teaching of Jesus being opposed to the teaching of Paul, and they say they accept the teaching of Jesus but not of Paul. They do not really accept either one. We need the teaching of Paul in order to understand some of the things our Saviour said. The Epistles become a divine commentary on what the Divine Teacher taught.

A common saying among men today is that we must have faith in ourselves. The Bible, on the other hand, tells us to have no confidence in the flesh. Paul says in Romans 7:18: "For I know that in me (that is, in my flesh,) dwelleth no good thing: for to will is present with me; but how to perform that which is good I find not." Paul had a renewed will but he needed more than that to live right and think right. He needed the right power and also divine revelation. Added to that he needed divine illumination in order to understand what God had revealed.

Perhaps we can illustrate the truth of illumination this way. When my son was in Bible school he would sometimes ask me questions concerning certain spiritual aspects of the Word of God. I would have to say to him time and again, "I can explain to you as the Lord has explained to me; but for it to become part of you, you will have to take time to wait on the Lord and let Him reveal it to your spirit by His Spirit."

This goes beyond mere head knowledge. Paul wrote to the Ephesians: "The God of our Lord Jesus Christ, the Father of glory, may give unto you the spirit of wisdom and revelation in the knowledge of him: The eyes of your understanding being enlightened; that ye may know. . . ." (Eph. 1:17). This is not a matter of head knowledge or mere human reasoning. It is a matter of knowing by the Spirit of God what these truths are and what they signify.

Paul an Exhibit of the Gospel

After setting forth the source of his gospel message, Paul presented himself as an example of what the gospel he preached had done for him. He says in Romans 1:16: "For I am not ashamed of the gospel of Christ: for it is the power of God unto salvation. . . ." This gospel does something for a person because it is the power of God in him. It is more than a mere set of regulations or a creed. It does something for us and in us. It changes us. This is Paul's argument.

The following portion from the Amplified makes this radiantly clear: "You have heard of my earlier career and former manner of life in the Jewish religion (Judaism), how I persecuted and abused the church of God furiously and extensively, and [with fanatical zeal did my best] to make havoc of it and destroy it. And [have heard how] I outstripped many of the men of my own generation among the people of my race, in [my advancement in study and observance of the laws of] Judaism, so extremely enthusiastic and zealous I was for the traditions of my ancestors" (Gal. 1:13,14).

The Galatians were familiar with Paul's life story. They knew from the standpoint of natural learning he was at the top. He stood high in academic circles. So far as zeal is concerned he outstripped his fellow religionists among the Pharisees. He showed this by his persecution of the Church, causing many Christians to be imprisoned and others to be put to death. Paul sincerely thought Jesus Christ was an imposter and sought to stamp out Christianity. He did all he could to oppose the preaching of the gospel, believing that Judaism was absolutely right. This was Paul's course of life until he met the Lord Jesus Christ and was completely changed. He did something for Paul no one else could have.

From man's standpoint Paul had every reason to have

confidence that what he was and what he did were sufficient to make him right before God. Writing to the Philippians he said: "For we are the circumcision, which worship God in the spirit, and rejoice in Christ Jesus, and have no confidence in the flesh. Though I might also have confidence in the flesh. If any other man thinketh that he hath whereof he might trust in the flesh, I more: Circumcised the eighth day, of the stock of Israel, of the tribe of Benjamin, an Hebrew of the Hebrews; as touching the law, a Pharisee; Concerning zeal, persecuting the church; touching the righteousness which is the law, blameless. But what things were gain to me, those I counted loss for Christ" (3:3-7).

According to what Paul tells us in this passage, no one had a better right than he to trust in his birth and upbringing and religious affiliation for personal salvation. He belonged to the strictest sect of the Israelites, that is, the Pharisees. He was meticulous in meeting all the requirements of the Law as the Pharisees interpreted it. But from the time he met and knew Christ as his life Paul changed his estimate of these things. He saw himself as a sinner and realized that Christ had died for his sins. Under the old system of Law Paul had thought he was blameless, but after meeting Christ he saw how wrong he was. He turned to Christ in faith, and his whole life and purpose and destiny were changed.

Paul continued narrating this experience in the following words: "But when it pleased God, who separated me from my mother's womb, and called me by his grace. To reveal his Son in me, that I might preach him among the heathen; immediately I conferred not with flesh and blood" (Gal. 1:15,16). It is surely significant that Paul said "to reveal his Son in me." God revealed Jesus Christ to Paul, and Christ became Paul's life. This meant that Paul in his preaching not only preached Christ by what he said but by what he was. His life was changed. He became not only a preacher of the Word but a living demonstration of God's life-producing grace. Someone has said, "The real life is in the indwelling Christ." This was thoroughly demonstrated in Paul because

Paul's life was changed from self-centeredness to Christ-centeredness.

Unless there is a change in our lives, a change which shows Christ living within us, there is real cause to fear that we have never really come to know Him at all.

In the remainder of this first chapter of Galatians the Apostle tells us that he did not confer or counsel with men after he received the revelation from the Lord Himself. He did not at that time compare what he received with the other Apostles to see what they might think or were teaching. God interpreted to him all that Christ did. It was made clear to the Apostle what Christ's death including His burial and resurrection signified and accomplished. It took a revelation from God to bring Paul to the place where he saw that Christ's death was redemptive. Christ's coming into the world was to do an atoning work for man.

The Judaizing teachers, as we have seen, attacked Paul's apostleship and attacked the gospel he preached. But their contention that he had not been sent out by the leaders of the church in Jerusalem and, therefore, was not an accredited messenger did not hold water. Paul was accredited by God Himself, and the authenticity of Paul's gospel was attested by the church leaders in Jerusalem. It was some three years after Paul was converted that he went to Jerusalem and spent about two weeks there with Peter. The only other leader he saw at that time was James, the Lord's brother. Yet during all this time he had been preaching the gospel on the basis of God's revelation to him. It is evident from this that Paul owed nothing to Peter or James with regard to the source and content of the gospel he preached.

Neither was Paul known by sight to the Christians in Judea. After his meeting with Peter and James he went on to Silicia and Syria. The Christians in Judea heard only "that he which persecuted us in time past now preacheth the faith which once he destroyed. And they glorified God in me" (Gal. 1:23,24).

Paul's Commission Recognized

It was 14 years later that Paul again went to Jerusalem taking Barnabas and Titus with him. Paul discussed with the leaders of the Christians the gospel he preached among the Gentiles, and the leaders "added nothing" to what he was teaching. Instead, "when they saw that the gospel of the uncircumcision was committed" to him, as "the gospel of the circumcision was unto Peter" they gave Paul and Barnabas the right hand of fellowship and endorsed their going to the Gentiles with the gospel.

In the conference Paul had with these men the decision was that the gospel God had given to Paul was identical with the gospel the others were preaching. Even though he had received it independent of men, it was the true gospel, for he had received it from the original source, the Spirit of God Himself.

In the great Council held in Jerusalem the subject discussed was whether or not Gentiles could be saved without the Law. Both Paul and Peter had part in this and Peter said, "Now therefore why tempt ye God, to put a yoke upon the neck of the disciples, which neither our fathers nor we were able to bear? But we believe that through the grace of the Lord Jesus Christ we shall be saved, even as they" (Acts 15:10,11). There is only one true gospel. It was the gospel Paul preached, the same gospel that Peter and the other Apostles preached.

James, the head of the Jerusalem church spoke up after it was evident the discussion was over and said, "Men and brethren, hearken unto me: Simeon [Peter] hath declared how God at the first did visit the Gentiles, to take out of them a people for his name" (Acts 15:14). The leaders, then, were all in agreement. They all preached the same gospel. They did not get it from each other. It was given by the Lord Himself.

This matter of the gospel of the grace of God without works was settled over 1900 years ago. But there are still teachers troubling the churches of today with the same corrupting doctrine, frustrating the grace of God and placing themselves under the curse of God. Let us hold to the liberty we have found in Christ and we will not be led astray by an imitation gospel.

Further proof that Paul's message was independent of men was Peter's failure to defend his actions when rebuked by Paul. Peter knew that men were not saved by keeping the Law or kept saved by means of it, yet he left off meeting with Gentile believers because they had not conformed with Jewish institutions. Peter had lived for awhile in such a way that he showed he did not believe that legal ordinances justified a man before God, Then, when certain Jewish Christians came from Jerusalem, he broke off contact with the Gentile believers and ate only with the Jews. This was to say by example that Gentiles must keep the ceremonial customs of the Jews. Peter's defection at this point was only temporary, but it was serious and others followed his hypocritical action also. Only Paul's clear understanding of the spiritual issues involved and his speaking out remedied the situation.

Paul went on to state that it was a matter fully known among Christians that a man is not justified by the works of the Law but by the faith of Jesus Christ. No flesh can hope to be justified by the works of the Law.

CHAPTER SEVEN

CRUCIFIED YET LIVING

This brings us now to one of the great statements in the Book of Galatians. It is found in 2:19-21. Verse 20 is the core of this passage, verse 19 is the foundation, and verse 21 is a capstone or roof for this entire section of truth. These three verses read in the King James Version as follows: "For I through the law am dead to the law, that I might live unto God. I am crucified with Christ: nevertheless I live; yet not I, but Christ liveth in me: and the life which I now live in the flesh I live by the faith of the Son of God, who loved me, and gave himself for me. I do not frustrate the grace of God: for if righteousness come by the law, then Christ is dead in vain."

Many concerned people keep asking, "Are we not under the Law? Surely there is some purpose for the Law in our lives." The answer to these matters is very clear from verse 19. There are three phrases used here and each one is vital in itself. First is "I, through the law"; the second is "am dead to the law"; and third "that I might live unto God." Here we have an execution, a death, burial and resurrection.

Paul says that the Law has already executed its sentence upon the believer. The sentence of the Law is death upon those who break it. And since none of us keep the Law even though we may try our level best to do so, the Law condemns all of us to death. Thus the Law sentences us and executes us. The one who does not keep the Law comes under the curse of the Law.

This is the statement of Galatians 3:10: "For as many as are of the works of the law are under the curse: for it is written, Cursed is every one that continueth not in all things which are written in the book of the law to do them."

There is no room to argue here. We cannot qualify as having lived a good life, so we came under the sentence of death from the Law. The Law itself is good, but we are unable to meet its requirements. Paul said in Romans 8:3: "For what the law could not do, in that it was weak through the flesh," shows where the problem lies. The Law is not weak but I am weak. Though the Law could tell me what to do, it could not give me the power to do it. Thus I come under the curse of the Law.

Christ Fulfilled the Law

Christ Jesus, however, fulfilled the Law completely. The Law could not curse Him, for He did not break it. However He bore our curse upon Himself. God made Him to be sin for us (II Cor. 5:21). Even though our Saviour was sinless He bore the responsibility of our sin in His own body so that we might be made the righteousness of God in Him.

Christ fulfilled the Law; then by dying He bore its curse upon Himself. Galatians 3:13 says: "Christ hath redeemed us from the curse of the law, being made a curse for us." And in Romans 8:3 the Apostle tells us that what the law could not do, God did through sending His Son in the likeness of sinful flesh and for sin condemned sin in the flesh.

Through our identification with Christ in His death, we have become dead to the Law. This is the witness of Romans 7:4: "Wherefore, my brethren, ye also are become dead to the law by the body of Christ." So then, we through the Law are dead to the Law. This is possible only because we have been identified with Christ in His death. Romans 6:3-5 says: "Know ye not, that so many of us as were baptized into Jesus Christ were baptized into his death? For if we have been planted together in the likeness of his death, we shall be also in the likeness of his resurrection." In verse 8 of the same chapter we read: "Now if we be dead with Christ." Proof again that we died together with Christ because of being united in Him.

Here is a man who has been arraigned in court for murder. He has been found guilty and the death penalty passed on him. Then the time comes that he is executed. When that takes place, the Law exacts its penalty and completes what it demanded.

The Father saw us identified with Christ as He hung on the cross. The Law did the executing, because the penalty of the Law is death for sin. So when Christ died, we died together with Him. And through this we died to the Law. Once a person is dead, the Law cannot execute that person again. Therefore, since we were identified with Christ in His death, we too have died to the Law.

Application to Christian Life

Now this fact has a very direct bearing on the Christian life. Because of our identification with Christ in His death we have died to the Law and also to sin. We are no longer under Law but under grace.

Paul proves this in the 7th chapter of Romans through the illustration of marriage. A man and woman are married according to the Law as long as both of them are alive. If the woman, for example, does not like her husband and cannot get along with him, her only hope of separation from him according to the law of marriage is that he might die. If he does, she is free from the law that binds her to him. Furthermore she is free from that law so that she can be married again.

It so happens, however, that the illustration Paul uses pictures the woman, not the husband, as dying. She, however, does not remain dead but is raised from the dead. Having died she is dead to the Law and is now free in her new life to marry another.

It is because of being dead to the Law that we can now live to God. And so the Apostle says, "I am crucified with Christ: nevertheless I live; yet not I, but Christ liveth in me." Romans 10:4 tells us: "For Christ is the end of the law for righteousness to every one that believeth." Or again as Romans 8:2 says, "For the law of the Spirit of life in Christ Jesus hath made me free from the law of sin and death."

Yes, Jesus Christ died, but He also rose again. Through

Him we have been brought forth from the dead. This is the truth of Colossians 3:1-3 where we learn that we have been raised together with our Lord. Ephesians 2:4-6 also tells us that we have been raised together with Christ Jesus.

Let us look once more at the illustration of the executed criminal. The Law condemned him and put him to death. But suppose through some miracle he was brought back again to life. What then? If someone were to meet him and report him to the authorities, demanding that he be executed again, all the law could say would be that it could not carry out the sentence. That person had been executed once and could not be executed the second time.

They tell the story of a soldier in Napoleon's army who was excused because of his large family. His brother went in his place and lost his life in one of the battles. Later on the father of the family was again called to take up arms but he objected on the basis of having died in the army in the person of his brother, and the courts upheld his position.

New Life in Christ

What is your estimate of your own Christian experience up to this point? Would it be that you have tried hard to please the Lord and you have failed? The solution to the problem very likely lies in understanding Galatians 2:20. We need to stop our struggling and let Christ do the living in us.

Our arms and legs when functioning properly do their work automatically. The reason is that they are part of the body, so the life of the body is in them and controls them. They do not have to struggle or try apart from the body itself. The signal to them is automatic and they respond.

This should be the way we live the Christian life. It is not up to us to do the living in our own strength. We need to let the life of the Lord work in and through us. What we need to exercise in this connection is faith; and it is to this that Paul makes reference when he says, "I am crucified with Christ: nevertheless I live; yet not I, but Christ liveth in me: and the life that I now live in the flesh [that is while we are here on this earth] I live by the faith [or the faithfulness] of the Son of God, who loved me, and gave himself for me."

The new life is life "in Christ." The word "in" does not in this connection speak of location such as "in an automobile" but carries the idea of union. We are in union with Christ. Through Him we are dead to the Law having been identified with Him in His death and resurrection. On the resurrection side of this experience we have His life. He has come to live in us. It is this that marks the real difference between the old life prior to our salvation and the new life now that we are saved.

It is necessary before the believer can enjoy victory in Christ for the power of the old life to be broken. This is accomplished through union with Christ in His crucifixion. This is not an experience that we must struggle to enter into now. It was accomplished for us in the past. The King James Version which most of us use is not clear on this point. The American Standard Version of 1901 will help us here. The expression, "I am crucified with Christ," is translated in the ASV: "I have been crucified with Christ." God got rid of the old self-life by crucifying it. We were separated from the old self-life when we died with Christ.

That this is past transaction is clearly demonstrated from Romans 6. In verse 2 Paul says, "We who died to sin, how shall we any longer live therein?" (ASV). In the third verse the Apostle says, "Know ye not that so many of us as were baptized into Jesus Christ were baptized into his death?" Here the verbs are clearly in the past tense and describe the finished transaction. Then in verse 5 we read: "For if we have become united with him in the likeness of his death, we shall be also in the likeness of his resurrection" (ASV). Again, in verse 7, the Apostle says, "For he that hath died is justified [released] from sin" (ASV). The past tense is also in verse 8: "But if we died with Christ, we believe that we shall also live with him" (ASV). So in the past is death, but in the present is life.

In his Letter to the Colossians Paul emphasized the same truth. He said, "For ye died, and your life is hid with Christ in God" (ASV). Or if we refer again to Paul's Letter to the Galatians he said in 5:24: "And they that are Christ's have crucified the flesh with the affections and lusts" (KJV). The flesh nature has been crucified. The self-life has been crucified. This is not something we do now.

On the other hand, what we have just seen from the Scriptures relates to the believer's standing or as some call it "position" before God. Our standing is how God sees us in Christ and that is a finished work, complete and without flaws. Now, in order to make victory possible in our everyday life, our walk, our condition on earth, we are to "reckon" ourselves "to be dead indeed unto sin, but alive unto God through Jesus Christ our Lord." We are to reckon that we have already died to sin. We are also to reckon that we are now alive to God through Christ. We count on the fact that we died to sin through union with Christ in His crucifixion, and we now live to Him because we are united with Him in His resurrection life.

Paul not only tells us in Galatians 2:20 that we "have been crucified with Christ," but adds, "nevertheless I live." We have died but we also live. How can this be? The Apostle explains, "Yet not I." It is not the old "I" who lives any more. There is a new life present. Salvation has brought a new creation. Death is past and life is present. Since we are risen with Christ we are to seek those things which are above. This is the very heart of Christian victory.

An Illustration

Perhaps we can illustrate it in the following manner. We are baptized in water after we believe. We are only baptized once, however. The subject of baptism is discussed in Romans 6:3,4 where water baptism is used as a picture of our being baptized by the Holy Spirit into the Body of Christ. Water baptism pictures our severance with the old life, the fact that we are finished with it and that we are satisfied with the new life in Christ. But we are baptized once, not again and again, since to do so would destroy the significance of the ordinance.

The Lord's Supper on the other hand we take often. The reason is that it pictures our continuous conformity to Christ's death. The Supper pictures the faith application of His death in our daily living. So far as God is concerned, in our position before Him in Christ, we have died once for all. This is pictured in baptism. I am daily, even momentarily, to reckon myself dead indeed unto sin. This is pictured in the Lord's Supper.

Paul makes reference to this phase of truth in Romans 6:11: "Likewise reckon ye also yourselves to be dead [to have died] indeed unto sin, but alive unto God through Jesus Christ our Lord. It is on the basis of this transaction, then, that the exhortation is made to us: "Let not sin therefore reign in your mortal body, that ye should obey it in the lusts thereof" (v. 12). Why not? Because we have died to sin and to the law and to the "old man." For this reason we must not yield our "members as instruments of unrighteousness unto sin," but we are to yield ourselves unto God "as those that are alive from the dead," and our members as instruments of righteousness unto God. In our position before God we have died to sin. In our condition on the earth the fallen sin nature is still with us and wants to control our bodies as before. However, through faith in Christ we can be victorious.

The formula for victory is presented in Ephesians 4:22-24: "That ye put off [have put off] concerning the former conversation the old man, which is corrupt according to the deceitful lusts; And be [Being] renewed in the spirit of your mind; And that ye put on [ye have put on] the new man, which after God is created in righteousness and true holiness." "The new man" is a regenerate man as distinguished from the "old man." The "new man" is a partaker of the divine nature and life. There is no sense in which the "old man" can be made over or improved. But with Christ now living in us, we will begin to manifest the fruit of the Spirit instead of the works of the flesh.

Same Personality But New Life

The Gospel of John tells us what happened when we were born again: "But as many as received him, to them gave he power to become the sons of God, even to them that believe on his name" (1:12). We did not just receive life from Him, we received Christ Himself. In fact, we have life because we have the Son.

When we want to have light in our homes we usually flip a light switch and the electrical current which comes from an outside source produces light in a bulb. This is not a parallel, however, to how we receive life from Christ. God does not in some way turn on a switch which connects to an invisible supply of life. This life does not emanate from God; it is Christ Himself. He indwells us and is our eternal life. This does not mean that we lose our personality. We are still the same individuals, but we now have Christ living in us and expressing Himself through our personalities. Before we were born again it was our old self born of Adam, with its sinful desires and lusts that characterized or controlled our personalities. Now all is changed since we have been born again.

This is a wonderful mystery now revealed according to Colossians 1:27, for it is Christ in us the hope of glory. The new life in us is a Person, the Lord Jesus Christ. According to Ephesians 2:10: "We are his workmanship, created in Christ Jesus unto good works." Though made up of only two letters the little word "in" is very important here as we have seen in previous Scriptures. It tells us that being "in" Christ Jesus is more than His indwelling us. It means that we are in union with Him. He takes control of our personalities making us Christ-centered individuals. Furthermore, it is no longer a human being seeking to draw near to God with the thought of establishing his human righteousness. God provides righteousness through Christ and produces in us righteous acts that please Him.

The holy and righteous life lived by the Christian is lived because of Christ living in Him. It is the expression of the new man who is created after righteousness and true holiness (Eph. 4:24).

It is no longer a matter of our trying to keep the rules and regulations of the law in our own strength. Rather it is a matter of yielding our personalities to the indwelling Christ. When we so yield, the Holy Spirit is able to work out God's purposes in and through us. The Holy Spirit indwells us as does Christ and forms Christ in us. In this way believers are energized in righteousness by the divine life resident within them. Christ is in us the hope of glory.

This great fact should help us see more clearly what Paul means in Philippians 2:12 when he says, "Work out your own salvation with fear and trembling. For it is God which worketh in you both to will and to do of his good pleasure." We cannot work out something that is not already in us. And in the working out of the salvation God has placed in us, our whole being will be involved—body, personality and spirit. This is why in Romans 12:1 we are exhorted to present our bodies to Him. We express ourselves through our bodies; so when these are yielded to God we are completely yielded to Him. Thus He can work out His purposes through us.

The Christ Who Indwells Us

Who is this Christ who indwells us? Do we realize the significance of the fact that the Greatest Personality of all time and eternity indwells each believer? In Hebrews 13:8 He is described as: "Jesus Christ the same yesterday, and to-day and for ever."

Look at some of His yesterdays. We read in John 1:3: "All things were made by him; and without him was not anything made that was made." He is the Creator of the universe. All things came into being through Him.

Paul said of Him in Colossians 1:16,17: "For by him were all things created, that are in heaven, and that are in the earth, visible and invisible, whether they be thrones, or dominions, or principalities, or powers: all things were created by him, and for him: And he is before all things, and by him all things consist." This is Jesus Christ who indwells us.

Consider now what He is today. We learn from the Scriptures that He is at the right hand of the Father. He is our Mediator in heaven, the Man Christ Jesus. At the very same time, however, since He is God He is omnipresent. That is, He is present everywhere at the same time. Though in His glorified body He sits at the right hand of the Father, at the same time He indwells each believer.

In Hebrews 1:3 we have proof of His present place in heaven: "Who being the brightness of his glory, and the express image of his person, and upholding all things by the word of his power, when he had by himself purged our sins, sat down at the right hand of the Majesty on high." Or as it says in Romans 8:34: "Who is he that condemneth? It is Christ that died, yea rather, that is risen again, who is even at the right hand of God, who also maketh intercession for us." He is our High Priest and Mediator representing us and praying for us before God the Father. There is none to compare to Him in God's universe for "God also hath highly exalted him, and given him a name which is above every name" (Phil. 2:9). Christ has authority which is above all other authorities. His is the final word. This is the Jesus Christ who dwells within us.

Let us consider Him now in His "for ever," the eternal future. There was time when He entered into history as the Babe in Bethlehem. This is the testimony of Isaiah to that great event: "For unto us a child is born, unto us a son is given: and the government shall be upon his shoulder: and his name shall be called Wonderful, Counsellor, The mighty God, The everlasting Father, The Prince of Peace. Of the increase of his government and peace there shall be no end, upon the throne of David, and upon his kingdom, to order it, and to establish it with judgment and with justice from henceforth even for ever" (9:6,7). Christ is today reigning in the heavens and He will reign in the universe for ever and ever. He reigns in the hearts of those of us who are believers, and there, too, He will reign for eternity.

What a privilege it is to be indwelt by this Saviour both now and for ever. He controls this world and the world to come. Is He controlling us at this moment? If not, there is something wrong with us. If we have been born again, He indwells us. If He is not controlling us, the fault lies with us.

Many of us know what it is to drive an automobile. Some cars are equipped with very powerful engines, some with less power; but regardless of the size of the engine, its power must be transmitted to the wheels before the car can move. If there is nothing there to transmit that power, the size of the engine will not help any. In the spiritual realm faith is the transmission between the power of the Lord Jesus Christ who indwells us and our day-by-day experience. If we do not trust Him for life and power from day to day, we will soon find that His power is not being transmitted into the activities of our lives. It is not enough that we believe *in Him* which may mean no more than belief in the fact that He lived in history. We must *believe Him*, take Him at His word and act according to His admonitions and promises.

Yes, I live, and yet "It is not 'I' but Christ" living in me. We must remember, then, to keep the self-life out of the way, for we have died to the old self but are alive to God. This is the key to the whole situation but the hardest fact for us to translate into experience. To reckon this true is the hardest step for us to take, but take it we must. Paul said in Philippians 3:7: "But what things were gain to me, those I counted loss for Christ." Then he went on to add: "Yea doubtless, and I count all things but loss for the excellency of the knowledge of Christ Jesus my Lord: for whom I have suffered the loss of all things, and do count them but dung, that I may win Christ."

Paul said concerning the practical side of the Christian life, "I die daily." By this he meant that he appropriated daily the fact that he had died to sin but was now alive to God. This was taught by our Saviour in these words: "If any man will come after me, let him deny himself, and take up his cross daily, and follow me" (Luke 9:23).

We live from day to day by the faith of the Son of God who loved us and gave Himself for us. We do not please Him by giving ourselves over to new laws or old ones or "better ones," but by appropriating His life by means of faith and depend upon His faithfulness. "Great is Thy Faithfulness." No wonder the Psalmist said: "Commit thy way unto the Lord; trust also in him; and he shall bring it to pass" (Ps. 37:5).

CHAPTER EIGHT

LIVING BY CHRIST'S FAITHFULNESS

Did you know that it is possible for a Christian to live without sin? Do not misunderstand. We have no reference here to what is known as sinless perfection. Some people claim that they do not sin any more, but this is not what we are speaking about. None of us so live the Christian life that we do not find it necessary to confess our sins to God daily. However, God has so provided for us in Christ that we need not sin.

The Lord Jesus Himself never sinned. He did not sin in thought or action or word or in any other way. Now, according to Galatians 2:20, the life we now live in the flesh we live by the faith or faithfulness of the Son of God who loved us and gave Himself for us. He is the Person who lives the new life in us. So a believer could live without sin if he constantly, both consciously and unconsciously appropriated the life of Christ and allowed Him to have perfect control over every thought, action or desire. In other words, if we would let the Lord Jesus control us as He controlled His own personality while on the earth, He would keep us in perfect control also.

This new life in us is dependent upon our having faith in Him or better counting on His faithfulness. We live "by the faithfulness of the Son of God" Paul says. So because I have faith or trust in Him, and because I depend totally on His faithfulness, the life which I now live in the flesh I live by Christ who indwells me. We say with Jeremiah: "Great is thy faithfulness" (Lam. 3:23).

Remember that in this Galatian letter Paul wrote to people who had been led from the path of truth and were following the pernicious teaching that the grace of God was not sufficient for a complete salvation. Law works, that is man's own righteous works, must be added both for salvation and for reaching maturity in Christian experience, the false teachers said.

Paul showed, however, that the Christian life is a life of faith. The word translated "faith" in Galatians 2:20 is many times translated "faithfulness." The context indicates which one it should be. Here it can be both. I am to have faith or trust in Him and to depend on His faithfulness to work in me both to will and to do of His good pleasure. When we commit our ways to Him, He makes things work out right for us according to Psalm 37:5. This is a portion of Scripture that God has blessed to my heart for many years. It can be applied in so many realms, such as the realm of leadership and the realm of daily living.

When we trust in the Lord and trust in His faithfulness, blessed results follow. The exhortation is, "Trust also in Him;" and the assurance is, "He shall bring it to pass." We need to trust Him who is in us.

Reckon

The word Paul uses to help us see this truth more clearly is the word "reckon." He says, "Likewise reckon ye also yourselves to be dead [to have died] indeed unto sin, but alive unto God through Jesus Christ our Lord" (Rom. 6:11). "To reckon" in the sense meant here is to "count something as a fact." Abraham believed God, we are told. He did not just believe in God but he believed God. He took God at His word. So in our case we are to reckon ourselves dead indeed to sin, or, more correctly, that we have died to sin and are alive unto God. Dying to sin is not something that we do now, for that has already taken place. We count it so in our daily experience. We both died in Christ and were resurrected in Him; consequently we should walk in newness of life.

Resurrection cannot take place until there has been a death. This we must remember to reckon on. We have died in Christ; now we are alive in Him. Since we have died to sin we are therefore admonished: "Let not sin therefore reign in your mortal body, that ye should obey it in the lust thereof."

So far as God is concerned we died to sin and sin has no right to rule over us in our daily experience. We are to reckon on this fact so that when temptation comes we simply say No to it. By the grace of God we are not merely going to live for Him sometime in the future, we are living for Him now and He is living in us. Because we are alive in Christ we are not to let sin reign in our bodies. We are alive unto God and He should reign and control us. According to Romans 8:2: "The law of the Spirit of life in Christ Jesus hath made me free from the law of sin and death."

Not Frustration of Law

This is a "by faith" life. Not a "by law" life. Paul makes a very strong statement at the end of this chapter in Galatians when he says, "I do not frustrate the grace of God: for if righteousness come by the law, then Christ is dead in vain." If we could save ourselves, and if we could live a righteous life by our own efforts, there was no purpose in Christ dying in the first place. He might as well have stayed alive.

The Amplified Version is very helpful here. "[Therefore, I do not treat God's gracious gift as something of minor importance and defeat its very purpose]; I do not set aside and invalidate and frustrate and nullify the grace (unmerited favor) of God. For if justification (righteousness, acquittal from guilt) comes through [observing the ritual of] the Law, then Christ the Messiah, died groundlessly and to no purpose and in vain.--His death was then wholly superfluous" (Gal. 2:21).

We cannot emphasize this too strongly.

Many things were in vain if the Law was necessary for salvation. Not only was Christ's sacrifice an unnecessary thing, but the sufferings of the Galatians because of their faith in Christ were also unnecessary if Judaism was the way of salvation (Gal. 3:4). Later on Paul said, "Christ is become of no effect unto you, whosoever of you are justified by the law" (Gal. 5:4).

We do not downgrade the Law when we put it in the place God has put it. But we frustrate the grace of God if we try to substitute Law for grace. When faith is given its proper place with grace, we find that a man is justified by faith without the deeds of the Law. The Law is not set aside by faith but is established. The Law was never given to save men's souls, so whatever being "established" means it is not that. The sinner establishes the Law by confessing his guilt and acknowledging he is justly condemned. Furthermore, by Christ assuming the sinner's place and enduring the penalty of the Law He establishes the Law. The Law is righteous and condemns the sinner to death. When that death takes place, the Law is satisfied. Christ through His death, then, established the Law.

Sometimes these truths do not come to us without a good deal of prayer and reflection; but even more is needed. Paul prayed for believers in Ephesians 1:17,18 that "the God of our Lord Jesus Christ, the Father of glory, may give unto you the spirit of wisdom and revelation in the knowledge of him: The eyes of your understanding being enlightened; that ye may know what is the hope of his calling." This is illumination. We must wait on the Holy Spirit and pray for Him to reveal these truths to our hearts and minds. He has already given them by revelation in the Bible; but for us to understand them we need spiritual enlightenment. This is why in the 3rd chapter of Ephesians Paul begins his prayer by stating: "That he would grant you, according to the riches of his glory, to be strengthened with might by his Spirit in the inner man" (v.16).

This is something that goes deeper than mere mental knowledge. It is beyond human reasoning or understanding. So Paul continued: "That Christ may dwell in your hearts by faith; that ye, being rooted and grounded in love, May be able to comprehend with all saints what is the breadth, and length, and depth, and height; And to know the love of Christ, which passeth knowledge, that ye might be filled with all the fulness of God" (Eph. 3:17-19).

What a life this is that God gives us in Christ! Love takes the place of law. God as to His nature is love, and He dwells in us and loves through us. The future of our spiritual life has potentialities that are unlimited.

Is the Spirit Received by Works or Faith?

Would it shock you to know that a good many people who have outwardly embraced Christianity will never get to heaven? This is an inescapable fact from what Paul tells us in Galatians. Dealing as he was with matters of life and death and eternity he wasted no words and held back no facts that showed the seriousness of this situation. He wrote to the Galatians: "O you poor and silly and thoughtless and unreflecting and senseless Galatians! Who has fascinated or bewitched or cast a spell over you, unto whom--right before your very eyes--Jesus Christ, the Messiah, was openly and graphically set forth and portrayed as crucified? Let me ask you this one question: Did you receive the (Holy) Spirit as the result of obeying the Law and doing its works or was it by hearing [the message of the Gospel] and believing [it]?-- Was it from observing a law of rituals or from a message of faith? Are you so foolish and so senseless and so silly? Having begun [your new life spiritually] with the (Holy) Spirit, are you now reaching perfection [by dependence] on the flesh?" (Gal. 3:1-3, Amp.).

Something had indeed gone wrong among the Galatian believers and many of them had been misled. It was at this very point, so crucial today in many areas, of the failure to distinguish between Law and grace or faith and works that the Galatians had been tripped up.

There is a definite place in the Christian life for works, never, however, as a means to salvation or as a means to keeping saved. Law demands works but grace requires faith and then produces fruit. If it is grace then it is by faith. But if it is of works or Law then grace and faith have no part. We have seen this before but it is something to keep before us constantly: "And if by grace, then it is no more of works: otherwise grace is no more grace. But if it be of works, then is it no more grace: otherwise work is no more work" (Rom. 11:6). Grace and works do not mix. If salvation is by works then it is not by faith. If it is of faith then it cannot be of works. The Apostle did not say that the Galatians were not saved, but he asked them how they were saved. As believers they had received the Holy Spirit, so the question logically was, did they receive the Holy Spirit when they believed or did they receive Him as a result of having kept the works of Law? Was it by faith or by human effort?

Ephesians 1:13 puts this question beyond all shadow of a doubt. "In whom [speaking of Jesus Christ] ye also trusted, after that ye heard the word of truth, the gospel of your salvation: in whom also after that ye believed [upon believing], ye were sealed with that holy Spirit of promise." It was upon their believing that the Spirit of God sealed these believers. That is, on the basis of faith the Spirit of God did this particular work on their behalf. Since that was the way the Christian life was begun—by faith—then do we now look to the Law to perfect what it took the Holy Spirit to begin? Do I look to the Law to finish what Christ has already finished? Remember, Hebrews 11:6 says that "without faith it is impossible to please God."

The Law does not save and cannot save. Paul tells us concerning Abraham in Romans 4: "For if Abraham were justified by works, he hath whereof to glory; but not before God. For what saith the Scripture? Abraham believed God, and it was counted unto him for righteousness" (vv. 2,3). Faith moves us into the favor of God: "Therefore being justified by faith, we have peace with God through our Lord Jesus Christ" (Rom. 5:1). Faith also claims the very life of God Himself: "He that hath the Son hath life; he that hath not the Son of God hath not life." It is faith that lays hold of God's faithfulness.

True Faith Results in Good Works

Faith also motivates to good works. True faith produces good works. This is the argument of James. He said, "Shew me thy faith without thy works, and I will shew thee my faith by my works" (Jas. 2:18). And he added, "Faith without works is dead."

If good works do not follow faith in Christ then we have the right to question if the person professing that faith has real faith and is saved. It is through faith that we receive justification or are declared righteous before God; and it is also through the exercise of faith after we are saved that good works are produced that please God.

According to Hebrews 11 faith works. It does not stand alone. "And what shall I more say? for the time would fail me to tell of Gideon, and of Barak, and of Samson, and of Jephthae; of David also, and Samuel, and of the prophets: Who through faith subdued kingdoms, wrought righteousness, obtained promises, stopped the mouths of lions, Quenched the violence of fire, escaped the edge of the sword, out of weakness were made strong, waxed valiant in fight, turned to flight the armies of the aliens" (vv. 32-34).

It took faith to produce all these works. Faith results in righteous deeds, but good deeds do not produce faith nor do good deeds produce salvation. Neither do good deeds in themselves make us better Christians. But when we are Christians, we will work works of righteousness because we are God's workmanship created in Christ Jesus unto good works. But these works will be wrought in the strength provided by the new life of Christ in us and will be under the direction of the Holy Spirit.

Another very crucial matter is brought to our attention in the question Paul asked the Galatian believers. He said: "Are ye so foolish? having begun in the Spirit, are ye now made perfect by the flesh?" Does the natural man bring the Christian to maturity? Of course not. In the same connection the Apostle asked: "He therefore that ministereth to you the Spirit, and worketh miracles among you, doeth he it by the works of the law, or by the hearing of faith?" What was the occasion of God's mighty workings in these areas? Was it due to the good works of the believers or His response to their trust in Him? The answer is obvious.

Abraham Believed God

The Apostle then referred them to Abraham and showed

that Abraham believed God and it was accounted to him for righteousness. He not only believed in God but he believed God. There is a difference. Even the devils (demons) believe in God. Only the fool says in his heart there is no God. But a man may believe in God and still be lost. There are many people today who have outwardly embraced Christianity. They say they believe in God, but have they believed God in the sense that Abraham did? To believe God means to take Him at His Word. It means to accept His Word at face value and trust His promises. This is what brings salvation—our believing God concerning Christ. This is true also in our sanctification, that is our separation from sin to God. When we believe that we have died to the old nature and that we are now alive to God, we have laid the ground work for a victorious Christian experience.

What did Abraham believe? According to Romans 4:18-22 Abraham believed what God told him about his son Isaac. The Lord said that Abraham would have a son and this son would be the father of many nations. But God's promises did not stop with Isaac. They went on to include Christ, for through Abraham's "seed" was the whole world to be blessed. This "seed," was, of course the Lord Jesus Himself (Gal. 3:16).

Abraham believed God concerning Christ, and it was this that God counted to him for righteousness. God asks us also to believe concerning Christ: "If we receive the witness of men, the witness of God is greater: for this is the witness of God which he hath testified of his Son. He that believeth on the Son of God hath the witness in himself: he that believeth not God hath made him a liar; because he believeth not the gospel that God gave of his Son. And this is the record, that God hath given to us eternal life, and this life is in his Son. He that hath the Son hath life; and he that hath not the Son of God hath not life" (I John 5:9-12). Abraham believed God to save him and that is what God asks us to do also.

It was 430 years after God made the special promise to Abraham that the Law covenant was made with Israel. It is clear from this, then, that Abraham could not have been saved by the Law. He could neither have been justified nor sanctified nor have had a perfect life of faith by following the requirements of the Law. This is why God gives the illustration of Abraham at this place in Romans. It demonstrates the folly of the argument that keeping the Law is necessary for salvation.

CHAPTER NINE

WHY CURSED FOR TRYING TO KEEP THE LAW?

Why is it that men are cursed by trying to keep the Law? That this is the case is evident from Galatians 3:10 which says, "For as many as are of the works of the law are under the curse: for it is written, Cursed is every one that continueth not in all things which are written in the book of the law to do them." This same verse in the Amplified is even clearer: "And all who depend on the Law—who are seeking to be justified by obedience to the Law of rituals—are under a curse and doomed to disappointment and destruction; for it is written in the Scriptures, Cursed (accursed, devoted to destruction, doomed to eternal punishment) be everyone who does not continue to abide (live and remain) by all the precepts and commands written in the book of the Law, and practise them."

Why is it that an individual is cursed even though he tries to do the best he can to meet the moral requirements of the Law? Because of this are we to regard the Ten Commandments which embody the highest possible moral standards regulating human conduct a curse? No, we are not calling the Law a curse. There is no higher rule of righteousness than the Law.

Where then does the curse lie that is spoken of in Galatians? The Law insists upon total obedience by men. There can be no deviation from its requirements. Consequently, any failure brings the condemnation of the Law. James says, "Whosoever shall keep the whole law, and yet offend in one point, is guilty of all." Perhaps we try and keep nine-tenths of it or even ninety-nine percent of it, but that percentage of failure is enough to bring the condemnation of the Law upon us. In breaking one part of the Law we are guilty of breaking the whole Law. So it is our inability to keep the Law that brings the curse of the Law upon us.

Now, then, if the Law itself is not cursed, and if the Law itself is absolutely good and its righteousness cannot be improved on, why is a man cursed if he tries to keep it?

The Law Shows Man to Be a Sinner

First of all, the nature and intent of the Law was not the way of salvation provided by God. It never was from the time Adam fell. The Law does not save. It shows man he is a sinner and needs a Saviour.

Galatians 3:19 is proof of this: "Wherefore then serveth the law? It was added because of transgressions." In his Letter to the Romans the Apostle taught the same truth: "Therefore by the deeds of the law there shall no flesh be justified in his sight: for by the law is the knowledge of sin" (3:20). In the 7th chapter of Romans, Paul says, "Was then that which is good [the law] made death unto me? God forbid. But sin, that it might appear sin, working death in me by that which is good [using law for this purpose]; that sin by the commandment might become exceeding sinful."

So far as its ministry to man is concerned, the Law does not bring life. Paul says of it in II Corinthians 3:7: "But if the ministration of death, written and engraven in stones, was glorious"—this is a direct reference to the Ten Commandments and they are called "the ministration of death." In verse 9 of the same chapter Paul describes the Law as "the ministration of condemnation."

Our Lord's Teaching on the Law

As a further background for answering our question, Why is a man cursed for trying to keep the Law? we need to consider what our Lord Himself taught concerning the Law and the keeping of it. A frequent answer people give who insist the Law has to do with salvation is that Christ kept the Law. In reality, this is not a reason for us keeping the Law for salvation because the Lord Himself was sinless, and He gave us insights into the Law that reveal how far short any of us come of keeping it.

In His Sermon on the Mount, the Lord showed that the infringement of the Law consisted not only in outward acts but in the sinful condition of the heart. He went further than any Jew ever went. He said it was not just a matter of keeping the letter of the Law but of not violating it either in desire or thought. He showed that even the most highly respected man might be a murderer or adulterer in God's sight because the keeping of the Law went further than just mere outward conformity. He said in Matthew 5:20: "Except your righteousness shall exceed the righteousness of the scribes and Pharisees, ye shall in no case enter into the kingdom of heaven." The scribes and Pharisees were the keepers of the Law in Israel in that day, but theirs was an outward conformity not an inward reality. Paul, who was a Pharisee for a number of years, said that from the standpoint of outward observances no one could point to him as a breaker of the Law.

The Lord emphatically taught that the outward observance is not enough because the Law deals with the very intent of the heart. He said, "Ye have heard that it was said by them of old time, Thou shalt not kill; and whosoever shall kill shall be in danger of the judgment: But I say unto you, That whosoever is angry with his brother without a cause shall be in danger of the judgment: and whosoever shall say to his brother, Raca, shall be in danger of the council: but whosoever shall say, Thou fool, shall be in danger of hell fire" (Matt. 5:21,22). It is clear from this that the Law strikes much deeper than mere outward acts.

The same is true concerning a subject that is all too prevalent today: "Ye have heard that it was said by them of old time, Thou shalt not commit adultery: But I say unto you, That whosoever looketh on a woman to lust after her hath committed adultery with her already in his heart" (Matt. 5:17,18). It is clear from this then that the thoughts and the intents of the heart are weighed by God, and this adds a new dimension to law keeping.

In his First General Epistle John wrote: "Whosoever

hateth his brother is a murderer: and ye know that no murderer hath eternal life abiding in him" (3:15). Hating one's brother makes a man a murderer. This is how strict the Law is. There is no leeway here.

So now ask yourself this question: Am I able to keep the Law? The answer is, no. None of us can. That is why we are cursed when we try to keep the Law. The Law itself is good but we are failures.

The Law's High Demands

An incident in our Lord's earthly ministry illustrates for us the exceedingly high requirements of the Law. "And, behold, a certain lawyer stood up, and tempted him, saying, Master, what shall I do to inherit eternal life? He said unto him, What is written in the law? how readest thou? And he answering said, Thou shalt love the Lord thy God with all thy heart, and with all thy soul, and with all thy strength, and with all thy mind; and thy neighbour as thyself. And he said unto him, Thou hast answered right: this do, and thou shalt live" (Luke 10:25-28).

Apparently the message got through to this man, for he promptly began to do some quibbling. But he could not avoid the force of what the Lord said. If a person does not love the Lord his God with all his might from the day of his birth to the day of his death, with all his soul and with all his strength, that one has failed. The Law accepts only one hundred percent obedience. Anything less brings its curse.

God knows this even though men have often shut their eyes to it. This is why God devised a method of salvation apart from law keeping. Paul wrote to the Galatians: "But that no man is justified by the law in the sight of God, it is evident: for, The just shall live by faith. And the law is not of faith: but, The man that doeth them shall live in them [if the law is to be the means of salvation then it must be kept perfectly]."

What was Christ's relation to the Law? He said this of it in His Sermon on the Mount: "Think not that I am come to destroy the law, or the prophets: I am not come to

destroy, but to fulfil" (Matt. 5:17,18). Christ's relation to the
Law, then, was that He was to fulfill it, not destroy it. He
went on to say, "For verily I say unto you, Till heaven and
earth pass, one jot or one tittle shall in no wise pass from the
law, till all be fulfilled." What is our hope of salvation if it
is not in keeping the Law? For the answer we turn again to
Galatians: "Christ hath redeemed us from the curse of the
law, being made a curse for us: for it is written, Cursed is
every one that hangeth on a tree" (Gal. 3:13).

Paul deals with this subject in Romans in these words:
"For what the law could not do [the law said 'Do this or
die' but could not make us behave], in that it was weak
through the flesh [we were weak], God sending his own Son
in the likeness of sinful flesh [made him sin for us], and for
sin, condemned sin in the flesh" (Rom. 8:3). So what men
could not do, Jesus did. He kept the Law, consequently the
Law could not condemn Him.

Yet God allowed Jesus Christ to stand under the condemnation of death and die, not because He deserved the
condemnation of the Law, but because He took our place.
He was delivered for our offences. It was our sins that nailed
Him to the cross.

The Time Element in the Law

The Law was given through Moses which was 430
years after God had given the plan of salvation to Abraham.
Now God did not set aside the plan of salvation even though
He brought in the Law. This matter is stated for us in Galatians 3:7-19: "Know and understand that it is [really]
the people [who live] by faith who are [the true] sons of
Abraham. And the Scripture, foreseeing that God would
justify—declare righteous, put in right standing with Himself—the Gentiles in consequence of faith, proclaimed the
Gospel [foretelling the glad tidings of a Savior long before-
hand] to Abraham in the promise, saying, In you shall all
the nations [of the earth] be blessed. So then, those who are
people of faith are blessed and made happy and favored by
God [as partners in fellowship] with the believing and trusting

Abraham. And all who depend on the Law—who are seeking to be justified by obedience to the Law of rituals—are under a curse and doomed to disappointment and destruction; for it is written in the Scriptures, Cursed (accursed, devoted to destruction, doomed to eternal punishment) be everyone who does not continue to abide (live and remain) by all the precepts and commands written in the book of the Law, and practise them.

"Now it is evident that no person is justified—declared righteous and brought into right standing with God—through the Law; for the Scripture says, The man in right standing with God (the just, the righteous) shall live by and out of faith, and he who through and by faith is declared righteous and in right standing with God shall live. But the Law does not rest on faith—does not require faith, has nothing to do with faith—for it itself says, He who does them (the things prescribed by the Law) shall live by them, [not by faith]. Christ purchased our freedom (redeeming us) from the curse (doom) of the Law's (condemnation), by [Himself] becoming a curse for us, for it is written [in the Scriptures], Cursed is everyone who hangs on a tree (is crucified); To the end that through [their receiving] Christ Jesus, the blessing [promised] to Abraham might come upon the Gentiles, so that we through faith might [all] receive [the realization of] the promise of the (Holy) Spirit.

"To speak in terms of human relations, brethren, [if] even a man makes a last will and testament [a merely human covenant], no one sets it aside or makes it void or adds to it, when once it has been drawn up and signed (ratified, confirmed). Now the promises (covenants, agreements) were decreed and made to Abraham and his Seed (his Offspring, his Heir). He (God) does not say, And to seeds (descendants, heirs), as if referring to many persons; but, And to your Seed (your Descendant, your Heir), obviously referring to one individual, Who is [none other than] Christ, the Messiah. This is my argument: The Law, which began four hundred and thirty years after the covenant [concerning the coming Messiah], does not and can not annul the covenant previously established (ratified) by God, so as to abolish the promise and make it void. For if the inheritance [of the promise depends on observing] the Law [as these false teachers would like you to believe], it no longer [depends] on the promise; however, God gave it to Abraham [as a free gift solely] by virtue of His promise.

"What then was the purpose of the Law? It was added—later on, after the promise, to disclose and expose to men their guilt—because of transgressions and [to make men more conscious of the sinfulness] of sin; and it was intended to be in effect until the Seed (the Descendant, the Heir) should come, to and concerning Whom the promise had been made. And it (the Law) was arranged and ordained and appointed through the instrumentality of angels [and was given] by the hand (in the person) of a go-between-an intermediary person (Moses) between God and man" (Amp.).

Israel utterly failed under the Law but their failure did not set aside the promise God gave to Abraham. The reason Israel is being brought back into the land today is that God promised them this in the Abrahamic Covenant. Israel has passed through a long time of chastening and discipline for their failure and the end of that is not yet in sight. But it is evident God is moving on their behalf and preparing a place for Christ's return to the earth. The promise, however, concerning grace and salvation which came to Abraham and which was on the basis of faith, was not submitted to the behavior test but was unconditional. But a behavior test was made when God added the Law 430 years after. Israel was put to the test and failed. God did not fail, however, and the unconditional promises He made to Abraham will be fully carried out.

We are assured by Paul in II Timothy 2:13 that God cannot deny Himself. He cannot fail: "If we believe not [if we are unfaithful as were the children of Israel under the law], yet he abideth faithful: he cannot deny himself."

CHAPTER TEN

THE SIGNIFICANCE OF THE LAW

Let us now consider some of the information given us in Galatians 3:19. We read: "Wherefore then serveth the law? It was added because of transgressions, till the seed should come to whom the promise was made." There are three important facts concerning the Law in this passage, and we will give each of them a close investigation.

The Law Had a Beginning

The passage before us says, that the Law "was added." It was added to something already existing. John the Baptist introduced our Lord to the public and said of Him: "The law was given by Moses, but grace and truth came by Jesus Christ." The Law had a definite beginning. It began not with Adam but with Moses. There was not a God-given Law in all that 2500 years or more between Adam and Moses, but there was sin and because there was sin there was death. Adam had some very definite instructions from God as to what he was to do or not to do, and he disobeyed. For this he died. But those who lived between Adam's day and the day of Moses died also, not because they had sinned exactly as Adam sinned but because they were sinners.

Sin was in the world before the Law came. This means then that Law had a definite beginning. It was added. But what was it added to? Adam, Noah, Abraham, Isaac, Jacob and all the others who were saved in those bygone years were saved by grace the same as we are today. Even during the Law period God always dealt with man in grace as far as salvation was concerned. God has only had one method of salvation before the Law, during the Law or after the Law.

The gospel is good news to all, past, present and future. But the Law was never good news. It was bad news. It was added to the good news but it did not take the place of grace. Neither was it mixed with grace. And it did not supplant grace. Grace was the good news but the Law was not.

The word translated "added," means "to place alongside of." The Law being placed alongside of grace does not mean grace was removed. This is wonderful to see and yet is all-important. Grace was there so that man could flee to it when the Law had done its work. When man saw himself condemned and cursed by the Law, he could turn to God's grace and find salvation.

Remember this was as true under Moses' Law as at any other time. No Israelite was ever saved by keeping the Law; they were saved only by grace. Thus Law was not added to grace but was placed alongside grace to show men their need of grace. The Law had a definite beginning in time. It was given through Moses about 1500 years before Christ and at least 2500 years after Adam.

Purpose of the Law

What then was the purpose of the Law? If the promise of grace was good, and it could not be disannuled, why bring in the Law? We have already seen that the Law was not given to make men better. It was not given to save them. What purpose could it then possibly serve? The answer is in Galatians 3:19. The Law was added because of transgressions. It was placed alongside grace in order to be transgressed. Men were sinners. They had been sinners all along from the time Adam fell. But the Law was given to make men transgressors. We recall again Romans 5:12,13: "Wherefore, as by one man sin entered into the world, and death by sin; so death passed upon all men, for that all have sinned: (For until the law sin was in the world: but sin is not imputed when there is no law.)" So the Law was brought in that it might be transgressed.

Law Reveals Men to Be Sinners

Sinning men needed the Law to reveal to them that they

were sinners and condemned because of law breaking. They thought they were all right, so they needed the Law spelled out for them in order that they would realize they were not all right. Not too many years ago though the State of Nebraska had a speed law, two of our neighboring states did not. One of them had a rather indefinite statement about traveling at reasonable rates. The other did not even have that. Suppose then that I traveled in one of those states at 75 miles an hour on a common road and was stopped by a policeman for speeding. He would have a difficult task making a case because there was no law that said I could not travel 75 miles an hour. There was no objective standard that I had broken. It might be that he would think my speed was unreasonable but that would be a mere opinion on his part. Since there was no written law that I had broken, he might find it very difficult to get a conviction. Yet he would very likely be right in concluding that my speed was unreasonable.

There are many things men do that are unreasonable and sinful, yet they need a written standard to show how wrong they are. They need something to prove that they are wrong and something that condemns them for doing the wrong. When men transgress it means they disobey. But if they disobey it is due to the fact they have something to disobey. It means they break or violate a law or command. So God brought in the Law to indicate how wrong sin is.

Though the Law was not present until the time of Moses, we learn that death reigned from Adam to Moses even over them who had not sinned in the way Adam had. Adam's sin was a transgression because he had a definite law from God. The Lord said to him, "Of every tree of the garden thou mayest freely eat: But of the tree of the knowledge of good and evil, thou shalt not eat of it: for in the day that thou eatest thereof thou shalt surely die" (Gen. 2:16,17). God gave a commandment and stated the penalty for breaking it. It was this that Adam transgressed. This also is the purpose of the Law. Between Adam and Moses men did not always have such biblical commands, so God says there was no transgression. Nevertheless there was sin and because of sin there was death. The Law was brought in to make sin a transgression.

Cain killed Abel but there was no law to apprehend Cain. There was no written law whereby someone could judge Cain or bring sentence upon him. The law concerning killing came later. Cain's murder of Abel was a sin, but there was no written law at that time to condemn that sin or to condemn the man who committed it.

Law Makes Men Conscious of Sin

The Law was also given in order to make men conscious of sin. The Law is a kind of spiritual mirror in which men can see themselves as they really are. The Law condemns men and brings them to an awareness of their need of grace. Unless men see how God considers wrongdoing, they will put their own value on their deeds, and sin to them will not seem sin at all. The Law brings men face to face with their sin and guilt: "Now we know that what things so ever the law saith, it saith to them that are under the law; that every mouth may be stopped, and all the world may become guilty before God. Therefore by the deeds of the law there shall no flesh be justified in his sight; for by the law is the knowledge of sin" (Rom. 3:19,20).

Sin which had always been present since Adam fell was morally wrong and is morally wrong. With the appearance of the Law sin becomes legally wrong. Sin is made a transgression by the Law.

Now, the Law did not produce sin, neither did it make sin worse. Furthermore, the Law itself was not sin. The Law was given to make sin appear what it really was—exceedingly sinful. It revealed the true nature of sin so that men might flee to God for grace.

It is possible for something to be morally wrong and yet legally right. In many areas of the country gambling is legalized. This makes it right in the eyes of the law. Nevertheless, it is still morally wrong. In the case of sin the Law came in and made sin legally wrong in order that punishment could be given.

Before the Civil War in the United States it was legal in some states to have slaves. But does that mean it was morally right? Of course not. Owning slaves is never morally right. So the Civil War was fought, in part at least, to decide whether slavery would be legally wrong or legally right.

During the first World War it was thought best in this country to have prohibition. So, prohibition was enacted into law. It became legally wrong then, not only morally wrong, to sell or buy liquor. Later on the 18th Amendment was repealed. Did that mean that it was no longer morally wrong to be a drinker of alcoholic beverages? It was just as wrong as it ever was even though now the traffic is legalized.

God found it necessary to give the Law so that that which was morally wrong would also be revealed as legally wrong in God's sight. It brought men to the place of condemnation through the Law in order that they could flee to grace and find salvation. This is part of the wonderful message in Romans 5:20: "Moreover the law entered, that the offence might abound. But where sin abounded, grace did much more abound."

The End of the Law

We learn from Galatians 3:19 that there was an end to the Law. There was a time when it began but there was also a time element with regard to its conclusion. It was given "till the seed should come to whom the promise was made." The promise was the promise of grace. The seed was Jesus Christ (3:16). Let us look again at verse 19 in the Amplified: "What then was the purpose of the Law? It was added—later on, after the promise, to disclose and expose to men their guilt—because of transgressions and [to make men more conscious of the sinfulness] of sin; and it was intended to be in effect until the Seed (the Descendant, the Heir) should come, to and concerning Whom the promise had been made. And it (the Law) was arranged and ordained and appointed through the instrumentality of angels [and was given] by the hand (in the person) of a go-between—an intermediary person (Moses) between God and man." Christ came at the appointed time. It is obvious that if the Law was given until the seed came, then the seed had an appointed time to come. This is also the record of Galatians 4:4,5: "But when the fulness of the time was come, God sent forth his Son, made of a woman, made under the law, To redeem them that were under the law, that we might receive the adoption of sons."

The Book of Hebrews testifies to this appointed time: "Above when he said, Sacrifice and offering and burnt-offerings and offering for sin thou wouldest not, neither hadst pleasure therein; which are offered by the law; Then said he, Lo, I come to do thy will, O God. He taketh away the first, that he may establish the second" (Heb. 10:8,9). The Law is considered first in this section. Being first it was removed in order that the second which is grace might be established. Under the Old Testament economy men's sins were covered but they were not put away until after Jesus came. Some 1500 years before Christ, the Law was given by Moses and was to remain until Christ Himself could come. Remember He came while the Law was still in force. He taught the Law. But He also taught grace. He taught the Law in order to make men see themselves as sinners. Many of them even then did not and would not see this truth. This was the reason the scribes and Pharisees hated Him so. They did not want to see themselves as He showed them to be.

Christ did not come to destroy the Law or the prophets but to fulfill. He promised that not till heaven and earth passed away would one jot or tittle in anywise pass from the Law until all was fulfilled. In fulfilling it He became the Lamb of God meeting the condemnation of the broken Law in our place. He fulfilled the Law by His obedience to it, and He fulfilled its demands by dying in our place. When the Law was fulfilled it was also finished.

The Apostle continues his discourse on this subject when he says, "But before faith came, we were kept under the law, shut up into the faith which should afterwards be revealed" (3:23). Then he shows the function of the Law in another respect when he says, "Wherefore the law was our schoolmaster to bring us unto Christ, that we might be justified by faith." The words "to bring us" are in italics which means they are not in the original. The passage should read: "Wherefore the law was our schoolmaster unto Christ." That tells us how long the Law was our schoolmaster. It was until Christ came. It was after that that we were justified by faith. After faith was come we were no longer under a schoolmaster or the Law. Thus the Law served as a trainer or guardian or guide to Christ. Through faith in Him we are justified or declared righteous, put in right standing with God.

Two Mountains

We have seen the purpose of the Law and the fact that there was a time element connected with it. The Law reveals sin, but since the Lord Jesus left we find God has another method of convincing men of sin. The Lord promised in John 16:7: "Nevertheless I tell you the truth; It is expedient for you that I go away: for if I go not away, the Comforter will not come unto you; but if I depart, I will send him unto you [this is the Holy Spirit]. And when he is come, he will reprove the world of sin, and of righteousness, and of judgment." The Law came by Moses but grace and truth came by Jesus Christ. The Law was given at Mount Sinai whereas Christ manifested God's grace on Mount Calvary. We see there the sinless, perfect Son of God hanging on the cross in terrible agony suffering not only physically but also spiritually, crushed under the load of our sins.

As I began to analyze this it was more than I could bear. Can you imagine what it means to have the sin of the whole world, past, present and future laid on Him? Let us look at Calvary and see the awfulness of sin—not His, but ours.

Mount Sinai condemns us. But Mount Calvary offers us pardon. Romans 8:1 says: "There is therefore now no condemnation to them that are in Christ Jesus." This covers our whole life. We learn that if we sin we return to God's fellowship through confessing our sins, "for He is faithful and just to forgive us our sins, and to cleanse us from all unrighteousness" (I John 1:9). God's will for us is, "My little children, these things write I unto you, that ye sin not. And if any man sin, we have an advocate with the Father, Jesus Christ the righteous." This is the story of Calvary as it works out for us. It is there we will realize the awfulness of sin. The Holy Spirit will take these truths to convict us and to bring us to Christ who alone can save.

However, if we have gotten past the stage of being convicted, and we are so calloused and hard that nothing seems to move us, it might be well for us to take a look again at the righteousness of God as revealed in the Law. Otherwise the Law has served its purpose.

Why the Offense in "Faith Alone"?

Why is the faith principle so offensive to man? Why don't men want it? Why do they revert back to the Law principle or the work principle when they consider salvation?

The answer is that to receive salvation by faith hurts man's pride. By doing law-works man gives himself reason to boast. But grace and faith allow no room for boasting whatsoever. Neither can our service for Christ give us any room for boasting. No matter how well we may serve Him we find that it is Christ in us Who is working out His purposes through us. There is no place for man to delight in himself in this.

The second reason for the faith principle being offensive to men is their ignorance of the grace of God. The Bible tells us that we are dead in sin. This is in our natural state. And the reason we cannot produce life of the kind that God asks is that such life comes only from Him. He is the source of it. Spiritual life cannot be generated by the natural man.

Now the Law does not reveal life. It reveals death. The Law tells us that we have sinned and that death is the consequence. Life comes only through Christ. This is the testimony of the Law and the prophets. "The righteousness of God without the law is manifested, being witnessed by the law and the prophets; Even the righteousness of God which is by faith of Jesus Christ unto all and upon all them that believe: for there is no difference" (Rom. 3:21,22). Just as

Adam received life from God, so must we receive life from God. And concerning this Jesus said, "I am the way, the truth, and the life: no man cometh unto the Father, but by me" (John 14:6). "He that hath the Son hath life; and he that hath not the Son of God hath not life" (I John 5:12).

The Law in God's Program Today

Let us now consider the place of the Law of God with regard to man today. *In the first place we have seen that the Law was dispensational.* Some will tell us they do not believe in dispensations, but they really do. There are some who have gone overboard on this matter, but the fact remains that the Bible is a dispensational Book. Anyone who believes the Bible at all believes that the Law had a beginning, for the Bible says so. They also know from the Bible that the Law had an end. The time between the beginning and the end of the Law is the Dispensation of the Law. The person who believes that Adam was in the Garden of Eden for a period of time and then sinned and was driven out, believes in the Dispensation of Innocence whether he calls it that or not. We are presently in the Dispensation of the Holy Spirit or The Church. The Law was dispensational. It began at Sinai and ended at Calvary. The Law came by Moses but grace and truth came by Jesus Christ. "The law was our schoolmaster . . . unto Christ, that we might be justified by faith. But after faith is come, we are no longer under a schoolmaster."

The Book of Romans tells us: "For Christ [means] the end of the [struggle] for righteousness [by the law] for everyone [who believes in him]" (10:4). Indeed this is wonderful! Righteousness is not through the Law but through faith in Christ and bestowed by God.

In the second place the Law was national. It was given to one nation only, not to the whole world. In Romans 2:12 we read: "For as many as have sinned without law shall also perish without law: and as many as have sinned in the law shall be judged by the law." Look also at verse 14: "For the Gentiles, *which have not the law,* do by nature the things contained in the law, these, having not the law, are a law unto themselves. So here we have two classes of people—one who received the Law and the other which did not have the Law.

The Apostle Paul reports this same truth from various angles. In Romans 9:4 he wrote: "Who are Israelites; to whom pertaineth the adoption, and the glory, and the covenants, *and the giving of the law."* Surely this is clear enough so that none would dare dispute it.

Or turn to Romans 3:19: "We know that what things soever the law saith, it saith to them who are under the law." There are those without the Law and those with the Law. It was national, given to Israel and not to the Gentiles.

In the third place the Law was given to demonstrate man's inability to make himself acceptable to God by his efforts. The Law is God's high standard. It cannot be lowered to accommodate man's low level. Never! Since it is God's high standard it reveals to man how far short he comes of the glory of God.

Man felt he was good enough to somehow please God. In order to disabuse men's minds of this God chose Israel to prove that man could not really please Him. There were no people on the earth that were so blessed and pampered as they were. They had the advantages of the best with which God could provide them. But in spite of all His provision for them they failed. Since a nation with all their advantages failed, what hope could there be for others who had no such advantages? None of them could qualify to become the children of God through their good works. This all emphasized man's necessity to come to Christ for salvation.

In the fourth place the Law had a special character of revelation. It revealed things. It showed man to be what he really is. Paul writes of this in Romans 7 where he declares: "For when we were in the flesh, the motions of sins, which were by the law, did work in our members to bring forth fruit unto death." The motions of sin were the activities of sin revealed in us. The Law reveals these activities. But by the Law also was the knowledge of sin. The Law did not cause sin but showed it up (Rom. 3:20).

In the fifth place the Bible shows that it is not possible for the Law to produce salvation and the full spiritual quality of life that follows. This is clear from Romans 8:3,4: "What the law could not do, in that it was weak through the flesh, God sending his own Son in the likeness of sinful flesh, and for sin, condemned sin in the flesh: That the righteousness of the law might be fulfilled in us, who walk not after the flesh, but after the Spirit."

So we see, then, that the Law could not do certain things. It could not make men behave themselves. It could tell them what they ought to do, but it could not provide them with the power to do so. It could not create righteousness.

Paul said of the Jews in Romans 10: "I know from experience what a passion for God they have; but, alas, it is not a passion based on knowledge. They do not know God's righteousness, and all the time they are going about trying to prove their own righteousness they have the wrong attitude to receive his. For Christ means the end of the struggle for righteousness-by-the-Law for everyone who believes in him" (vv. 2-4, Phillips).

The Law revealed the unrighteousness of man. There was nothing wrong with the Law, but there was much wrong with man. The Law itself has a righteous quality, and when we trust in Christ, the righteousness of the Law may be fulfilled in us but not until then. The Scriptures do not say that the righteousness of the Law will be "fulfilled by us," but "in us" because it is something the Spirit of God does. This is the sanctification of the Christian life. It is a complete change from within and not merely outward behavior. When we are led by the Spirit of God, this is realized in our everyday experience.

We are not under the Covenant of Law today. We go to Calvary to find the law of Christ; and the indwelling Christ through the Holy Spirit produces the good works "which God has before ordained that we should walk in them."

CHAPTER ELEVEN

SON OR SERVANT?

The subjects of law and grace are approached from a number of different aspects in the Book of Galatians. For example, in the first part of chapter 4 these truths are illustrated by comparing the relationship of a servant with that of the heir-apparent. For the first few years in the heir's life, as long as he is in his minority, he is under tutors and governors and is as much under the direction of others as is a slave in the household. But there comes a day when the son reaches maturity and he is given the place of a full-grown son in the home.

In our cultures this might compare to the time when a son or a daughter is married and leaves the father's house to establish another home. As long as a child in the home puts his feet under the family table, he is under the rules and regulations of the home, but with maturity comes a new relationship. This is the lesson that is carried over into the spiritual realm to illustrate our changed relationship to the Law through Christ.

Paul says, "Now I say, That the heir, as long as he is a child, differeth nothing from a servant, though he be lord of all; But is under tutors and governors until the time appointed of the father. Even so we, when we were children, were in bondage under the elements of the world: But when the fulness of the time was come, God sent forth his Son, made of a woman, made under the law, To redeem them that were under the law, that we might receive the adoption of sons. And because ye are sons, God hath sent forth the Spirit of his Son into your hearts, crying, Abba Father. Wherefore thou art no more a servant, but a son; and if a son, then an heir of God through Christ" (Gal. 4:1-7).

This passage tells us of Christ's relationship to man. He was God the Creator as well as God the Son. But the Father sent Him forth "made of a woman." Jesus Christ came into this world not only with a human body but with a sinless human nature. The time He came was during the dispensation of Law. This was no accident. This was all in the design of God. Our Lord came into the world while Israel was still under the Covenant of Law which began with Moses and ended on Calvary when our Lord died. When He arose from the grave, He was no longer under Law.

The Saviour came to show the real meaning of the Law and to counteract its judgment of death. The Law was given to show men that they are sinners, but Christ Himself was sinless. He kept the Law perfectly. No one could point the finger at Him as being guilty of having broken the Law in any part. So He fulfilled its moral and spiritual requirements, and then died on behalf of us who were condemned to death because of breaking the Law. He died for our sins.

Mature Sons

This is the intent of verse 5 which tells us He came to redeem them that were under the Law. But the same verse tells us He also came "that we might receive the adoption of sons." This takes us back to the illustration we began with. He came to redeem us, and He also came to give us a place as mature sons before God. He wanted us to have the life of God so that we might be able to live as victors over sin. Christ does this by living His life through us.

We not only were placed as sons but because we are sons, God sent His Spirit into our hearts crying "Abba, Father" or "Dear Father."

The Law could not give us power. It can tell us what is wrong with us but we need the Holy Spirit, whom God has sent into our hearts, to give us life and power. Since we are sons and in need of help, we can speak to the Father as a son to his father. He has already given us His Son Jesus Christ; therefore, the Father will not withhold anything else we need. With Him who was given on the cross for us, God will also give us all things. This He will do freely, for we are His heirs. We have an inheritance from Him.

We learn in Ephesians 1:14 that the Holy Spirit who now indwells us is the earnest of our inheritance until the redemption of the purchased possession.

The Apostle tells us in II Corinthians 3:5: "Not that we are sufficient of ourselves to think any thing as of ourselves; but our sufficiency is of God." All this help comes from God. We are utterly helpless without Him. God's blessings come through Christ according to Colossians 2:9,10: "In him dwelleth all the fulness of the Godhead bodily. And ye are complete in him, which is the head of all principality and power."

In the light of all of this how tragic it is for one to belong to the royal family of God and still serve in the spirit of a slave. When any of us who are believers in Christ put ourselves under the Law, we put ourselves in the place of slaves. As God's children through faith in Christ there is freedom for us from the Law, not bondage to it. This was Paul's argument in Galatians 4:9: "But now, after that ye have known God, or rather are known of God, how turn ye again to the weak and beggarly elements, whereunto ye desire again to be in bondage?"

What Enslaves Us Today?

Let us bring this down to where we live. What enslaves us today? We see men around us enslaved by alcohol and tobacco; enslaved to the self-life; enslaved by quick temper; enslaved by church ritual or tradition; or enslaved to the habit of trying to do things for themselves that only Christ can do. The Law cannot deliver us from these things, but Christ can: "For Christ is the end of the struggle for righteousness-by-the-law" (Rom. 10:4, Phillips).

Having been set free, we are to follow the Lord on the same principle of faith by which we received Him. Colossians 2:6 says, "As ye have therefore received Christ Jesus the Lord, so walk ye in him." We received Him by faith and we continue to walk in Him by faith. We become children of God through faith, and we keep on believing throughout our Christian experience for victory.

To lose this aspect of daily living by faith is to lose the likeness of Christ in our conduct and character. This is why Paul prays according to verse 19 of Galatians 4: "My little children, of whom I travail in birth again until Christ be formed in you." This is done not by our obedience to any system of law but through the faith life, allowing the life of Christ to be developed in us.

Two Covenants

The last part of the chapter is given over to an illustration from the family life of Abraham. Once again we have an answer to the question, "Is the believer under the Law?" Paul uses this bit of actual history to illustrate divine truth fitted for immature believers who had been confused by legalistic teachers.

The Apostle wrote: "Tell me, ye that desire to be under the law, do ye not hear the law? For it is written, that Abraham had two sons, the one by a bondmaid, the other by a freewoman. But he who was of the bondwoman was born after the flesh; but he of the freewoman was by promise. Which things are an allegory: for these are the two covenants; the one from the mount Sinai, which gendereth to bondage, which is Agar. For this Agar is mount Sinai in Arabia, and answereth to Jerusalem which now is, and is in bondage with her children. But Jerusalem which is above is free, which is the mother of us all" (Gal. 4:21-26).

We have a series of twos in this allegorical illustration. The two wives of Abraham are mentioned here—one a slave woman, the other a freewoman. There are two sons—Ishmael born to Hagar the slave woman, and Isaac born to Sarah the freewoman. Two covenants are represented, the covenant of the Law and the covenant of grace. Two mountains are mentioned, Mount Sinai and Mount Calvary—the former the Mount of the Law, and the latter the Mountain of the cross. There are also two cities named, the earthly Jerusalem and the heavenly Jerusalem.

What is the explanation of these things? God promised Abraham and Sarah a son, but after years of waiting, when it seemed as though the promises of God would never be realized, Sarah decided something needed to be done. She persuaded Abraham to marry Hagar, an Egyptian slave belonging to Sarah. Sarah's purpose was to have this young woman bear a child that she, Sarah, could claim as hers. Ishmael was the son born to Hagar.

Some 14 years later Isaac was born to Sarah. This precipitated a crisis in the home. By trying to help God out Abraham had resorted to human ways. This is represented in our allegory as Ishmael being born "of the flesh." And he actually represents the work of the flesh in this illustration. The flesh, as we have seen, God will not and cannot accept. Isaac on the other hand, was born according to God's promise. The child was born when neither Abraham nor Sarah were physically capable of being the parents of a child. It was then that God stepped in and fulfilled His promise through His divine power.

The lesson God has for us here is that we cannot ever fulfill the commandments of God by our own human efforts. They can only be kept as we accept Christ as Saviour. Then, through the indwelling Spirit, the life of Christ is fulfilled in us. The bringing of Ishmael into the world was all of man's planning. God had nothing to do with it. That which is of the flesh displeases God and He will not accept it. Ishmael was a child born after the flesh; and since his mother was a slave, he too was a slave.

With Isaac it was entirely different. He was born of a freewoman. His coming into the world was due to God's work. So the point made here is that we are considered through faith in Christ to be the brethern of Isaac. We are the children of promise born through divine power and not through human effort.

Further truth is also seen here: "But as then he that was born after the flesh persecuted him that was born after the Spirit, even so it is now." When Isaac was growing up, Ishmael was jealous of him and began to persecute him. This is what precipitated the crisis in the home of Abraham. The remarkable fact is that in the posterity of these two sons, the Arabs, the descendants of Ishmael and the Israelites, the descendants of Isaac, this enmity still exists.

But there is still another enmity involved. This is something that affects the Christian, therefore it is tied in with the two things represented by Ishmael and Isaac, namely, Law and grace. There is a strong tendency on the part of those who insist that Law is necessary for salvation to persecute those who preach salvation by grace plus nothing. Those who insist on Law say that we who preach grace are making it easier for people to sin. But this is not the case. Grace does not give men license to sin. It teaches us to deny ungodliness and worldly lusts and to live soberly and righteously in this world. So even though opposition or even persecution come, we should be ready to endure them.

But what is to be our attitude in this teaching of Law and grace? Are we to go along with the teachers of Law and say nothing? The answer of Scripture is, "Cast out the bondwoman and her son: for the son of the bondwoman shall not be heir to the son of the freewoman." The two will not mix. We are saved by grace. We are not in bondage to the Law. We cast it from us.

CHAPTER TWELVE

STANDING FAST IN LIBERTY

The first two chapters in the Book of Galatians contains Paul's defense of his apostleship. The next two chapters are doctrinal, showing that the Law cannot justify us, neither can it sanctify us. The fourth chapter concludes with the glorious truth that believers in Christ Jesus "are not children of the bondwoman, but of the free." We have been delivered from the curse of the Law and are therefore enjoined to conduct ourselves in a certain way as a result. The first words in chapter 5 are: "Stand fast therefore in the liberty wherewith Christ has made us free, and be not entangled again with the yoke of bondage." This marks the turning point from doctrine to duty or to privilege. It takes in all that has preceded by way of doctrine and focuses our attention on practical day-by-day living.

It is heart-rending to see so much failure in practical Christian living among God's people. This need not be. There is a great deal of emphasis today upon action and this idea is quite widely carried over into the everyday activity of Christians. It is do, do, do, until we forget what Christ has done and is still doing for us. Christians ought to be active but the purpose for the activity must be scriptural. We may tell a child that he has to do something or the consequences will be severe for him. He might obey out of fear, but how much better when he obeys out of love. We who are believers are in God's family and our obedience to the Lord should spring from what we are, not from fear of the consequences if we do not obey Him.

Today's society is full of problems. We all have unsolved problems of our own, and it is common among us as believers to say that the solution to all problems lies in Christ. Chapters 5 and 6 of Galatians bear this out. They consider many and point us to Christ as the answer for all of them.

It is as free individuals that we obey God. Paul tells us in Romans: "The law [principle] of the spirit of life in Christ Jesus hath made me free from the law [principle] of sin and death." Through the Law we are dead to the Law according to Galatians 2:19. We are delivered from the Law according to Romans 7:6. So we have been made free to obey God. Salvation by grace means just such deliverance and freedom.

We have to stand fast in the liberty wherewith Christ has made us free. Let it be pointed out again that Christian liberty is not liberty to sin. In these United States of America we have a government and a constitution which provide us with a great deal of liberty as compared to many other countries. We have freedom of speech, freedom of religion, freedom of the press to mention only a few. But how far can we take these liberties? At the present time we are experiencing a certain amount of anarchy. Can we carry our liberties to the place where it is all right for us to revolt against the established government? Of course not!

The Apostle answers this question concerning freedom in Galatians 5:13. He says, "Brethren, ye have been called unto liberty; only use not liberty for an occasion to the flesh, but by love serve one another." We are not to let our freedom become an opportunity for our lower natures to take over. We are free to serve each other in love.

Since we are saved by grace can we do what we want to? Think carefully—as saved individuals, as God's children saved by grace, can we do as we want to? The answer is an emphatic Yes. A genuinely saved person can do exactly what he wants to, remembering that the saved person has been given by God a different "want to." When the Christian is controlled by the Holy Spirit, his will is to do the will of God. The believer is not what he once was. He has been freed from the flesh so that he can live pleasing to God. Paul tells us in II Corinthians 5:17: "If any man be in Christ, he is a new creature: old things are passed away; behold, all things are become new." What things are become new? Our desires for one thing. Our "want to" is new.

We read in Romans 5:5 that hope maketh not ashamed, "because the love of God is shed abroad in our hearts by the Holy Ghost." The same love that caused God to send His son into the world to die for us has been shed abroad in our hearts by the Holy Spirit. This brings a change in our disposition and desires. This is why Paul can say in II Corinthians 5:14: "For the love of Christ constraineth us." It pulls us in a new direction. It makes us want to do the things that please God. Peter tells us that we have been made partakers of God's nature (II Peter 1:4). If there is no such change, there is no salvation.

Now sin has not passed away but the old ways of doing things, the old desires and longings are changed. God works in us both to will and to do of His good pleasure (Phil. 2:13). There must first be a "wanting to" before there can be a doing. He must want righteousness before we can do righteous deeds. God makes it possible for both to be true in us.

Before we were saved, we had only the flesh nature dominating us. But when we trusted Christ, the Spirit of God came in. Now we learn: "The flesh lusteth against the Spirit, and the Spirit against the flesh: and these are contrary the one to the other: so that ye cannot do the things that ye would" (Gal. 5:17). All of us who have trusted in Christ are conscious of the battle that began as the flesh opposed the Spirit and the Spirit of God sought to lead us into paths of righteousness. The battle, however, is the Lord's and He will give us the victory.

What Is Christian Liberty?

Christian liberty is liberty or freedom from the condemnation and eternal punishment of sin. It is also liberty or freedom from the enslavement and power of sin. These two aspects of liberty are beautifully illustrated for us in the experience of Israel. The people of Israel were slaves in Egypt and called on God for help. He sent Moses to deliver them. A number of severe judgments were visited upon the land and the people of Egypt, the final one being the slaying of the firstborn. God told the Israelites, however, that they could have a substitute so that the firstborn member of the family would not die. They were told to take a lamb, sprinkle the blood on the door posts and the death angel seeing the blood applied to the house would not slay the firstborn in it. Thus the Israelites were saved from judgment.

A second step in their redemption was taken when they came to the Red Sea. They crossed over through the miraculous deliverance of God and came out victorious on the other side. The Egyptians who dared to follow them into the sea were drowned and the power of Egypt's army was broken. Pharaoh and his rulers were buried in the waters. The power of slavery was broken for the Israelites. Not only were they set free by a substitute from the judgment of the death of the firstborn, they were also delivered from the power of Egypt when Egypt's army was destroyed.

This illustrates for us the truth of deliverance from the judgment of sin and also the power and enslavement of sin in the daily life. The people of Israel allowed themselves to be enslaved at a later time but never again by Egypt.

Christian liberty means more, however, than these. It means we are set free to partake of and enjoy the blessed life in Christ Jesus. We are free to enjoy access to all that God has for us in Christ. Paul tells us in Ephesians 1:3 that God has blessed us in all spiritual blessings in heavenly places in Christ Jesus. The same Apostle wrote to the Romans: "He that spared not his own Son, but delivered him up for us all, how shall he not with him also freely give us all things?" (Rom. 8:32). We have access by faith into the grace wherein we stand according to Romans 5:2. There is no lack for us who trust in Christ. And in case these passages are not enough to convince us, here is what Paul said to the Corinthians: "God is able to make all grace abound toward you; that ye, having all sufficiency in all things, may abound unto every good work" (II Cor. 9:8). It is in this liberty that we are to stand fast.

Christian Liberty in Romans

Christian liberty is set forth in the 6th chapter of Romans. Here we are told we are not under law but under grace, and as a consequence we should be so yielded to the Lord that our bodies express righteous acts and not evil deeds.

Chapter 7 tells of the experience of Paul in which he became entangled with the Law again. It brought on a time of intense spiritual struggle and ended in bondage. He found himself wanting to do the right thing but doing the wrong thing. He found there was no good in his flesh nature. He had the will to please God but had not found the method. Then the truth burst on him that deliverance and victory lay in Christ.

The 8th chapter of Romans declares true liberty. It presents the walk of the Christian based on the principle of the life of Christ in us as administered by the Holy Spirit. Paul used the illustration of the Israelites in the 10th chapter of Romans to demonstrate how persons with a great zeal not based on knowledge can go astray. Instead of receiving God's righteousness, the Israelites went about to establish their own righteousness, but in spite of all their struggles they failed. They did not realize the truth that Christ means the end of the struggle for righteousness.

Faith That Works By Love

The key to this whole situation lies in the little word "faith." This is not faith in one's self as some people try to tell us. It is true that there are certain areas in life in which there must be a certain amount of self-confidence if we are to meet our responsibilities. But, when we come into the spiritual realm, it is not a matter of self-confidence. It is faith in Him alone. As we have received Him by faith so are we to walk in Him by faith.

According to Galatians 5:5 we through the Spirit wait for the hope of righteousness by faith. We wait for it to be worked out in us, and we wait in faith. The following verse says, "For in Jesus Christ neither circumcision availeth anything, nor uncircumcision; but faith which worketh by love."

This statement, "faith which worketh by love," is very important. Saving faith is the kind of faith that works. It does something. It motivates, it creates new desires within us, and makes us want to please God. Good works did not produce this faith, but faith produces good works.

James wrote: "What doth it profit, my brethren, though a man say he hath faith, and have not works? can [that] faith save him?" (2:14). Faith that has no good works following it is not saving faith. A faith that does not produce righteous works is not faith from God.

Furthermore, faith works by love, not by law. The law says to me, "You must do this," and so I try to do it. This approach goes at the whole thing backward. The Law says that I must have works, therefore I must have faith, therefore I must have love. It begins from the other direction. The motivating power, the constraining power is in Christ and is expressed in us. Love is implanted in us through the Holy Spirit. It is love that controls us and urges us on. But the motivating power and the strength to do it comes from God. Colossians 1:29 in the Amplified reads: "For this I labor . . . striving with all the superhuman energy which He so mightily enkindles and works within me." Philippians 4:13 says, "I can do all things through Christ which strengtheneth me." In the Amplified this reads: "I have strength for all things in Christ Who empowers me—I am ready for anything and equal to anything through Him Who infuses inner strength into me, [that is, I am self-sufficient in Christ's sufficiency]."

Love Fulfills the Law

Love is the fulfilling of the Law according to Galatians 5:14: "For all the law is fulfilled in one word, even in this; Thou shalt love thy neighbor as thyself." This is impossible to us apart from Christ who has shed this love abroad in our hearts by the Holy Spirit. Moreover, He indwells us in order to empower us to express His love. Love goes beyond the

Law. The Law says we must do certain things, so we may try to do what is required, but nothing more. With this kind of attitude we never do more than we have to. Love, on the other hand, knows no such limitations and goes far beyond the Law in getting our response in things of righteousness.

Those who charge that our liberty in Christ produces looseness of living and license to sin do not know the power of grace. It is evident that they have not tried it.

Servants in the home are bound in the very nature of the case to follow rules and regulations. They work for certain hours and do certain things and in this way meet their obligations to their employers. But take my situation where we do not have a servant. My wife keeps the home. We love each other and have been married for many years. Do you suppose that when I leave for a week or two, as I sometimes do in the course of my ministry, that I lay down a number of rules for my wife to follow in my absence?

Or while I am at home can you imagine me setting rules for her to follow with regard to her household duties? Of course not! She serves and works because of love. She often spends more hours than I think she ought to. Because she must? No, but because she loves. When we by faith have received Jesus Christ, He changes our attitude so that there is within us an impelling love. This is what urges us on to serve the Lord.

What then is a believer's attitude toward the Law? Must he keep it? No! There is nothing in the Bible that says we have to keep the Law. Nevertheless, a born-again believer desires to show in his conduct the righteousness that is in the Law. He wants to do this not because he has to, but because He is indwelt by Christ who kept the Law perfectly. The outworking of the life of Christ creates the desire to uphold the righteous standards inherent in the Law.

One never forces a tree to bear fruit by the exercise of law. We do not set up a group of rules and regulations for a tree to follow in order to produce fruit. A healthy tree under proper conditions will bear fruit if it is properly watered and fertilized. So the regenerated Christian who is controlled by the Holy Spirit will bear fruit. There must be proper conditioning, of course, and this may be the clue to our not being as successful as we should. Perhaps we are not feeding ourselves on the Word of God. Perhaps we are not believing Him for the fulfillment of His promises.

So we are to stand fast in the liberty wherewith Christ has made us free. We are free from the Law. We are also free from entanglements and free from the power and slavery of sin. We are free to enjoy all that the life of Christ has provided for us.

The problem in the Galatian church was that the Christians believed they had to get back under the law of circumcision. Paul wrote to them, "I Paul say unto you, that if ye be circumcised, Christ shall profit you nothing" (5:2). This aspect of the law involving circumcision may not affect us today, but any attempt to get back under the Law in any way turns off the power of Christ. It is just like turning off a light switch. When we turn it off the connection with the power is broken.

A soldier sent out into battle who cuts himself off from his company and the line of supplies will not last long. In 5:4 Paul wrote: "Christ is become of no effect unto you, whosoever of you are justified by the law; ye are fallen from grace." Here is the way the Phillips translation renders this verse: "If you try to be justified by the Law you automatically cut yourself off from the power of Christ; you put yourself outside the range of his grace." Some have a very superficial concept of grace. They think God "helps those who help themselves." But this is not God's method. In the spiritual realm there are two methods God uses in dealing with man. Under the Law He condemns him, but under grace Christ becomes all to us—all that we need.

Can One Fall From Grace?

What did Paul mean when he said that certain Christians had fallen from grace? He meant that they had fallen out of God's favor. They gave up God's provision for their needs.

As we have already indicated, a great many persons have a superficial concept of grace. To them it is something that braces them up a little, that helps them when they are in need. But this view is totally inadequate. Grace is not a temporary stimulant but an all-comprehensive principle of God's dealing with us.

Many people, even Christians, depend upon their own will power to get them out of difficulties. They believe that they can take care of themselves and need no outside help. This is contrary to God's way of life in the spiritual realm. "It is God which worketh in you both to will and to do of his good pleasure" (Phil. 2:13), is the Apostle's declaration in this area. This is how God's grace works. By trying to do the best we can, we cut ourselves off from the supply line of grace from God.

A number of Scriptures tell us how God has given us adequate means to supply every need. For example, righteousness comes from God when we exercise faith: "For we through the Spirit wait for the hope of righteousness by faith" (Gal. 5:5).

In Romans the Apostle Paul goes into more detail in this matter. In 8:11 he says: "But if the Spirit of him that raised up Jesus from the dead dwell in you, he that raised up Christ from the dead shall also quicken your mortal bodies by his Spirit that dwelleth in you." The subject here is not a future physical resurrection. The Apostle is telling us about a spiritual resurrection in the present experience of the believer, the manifestation of the new life of Christ in us. Again he says, "But if ye through the Spirit do mortify [make to die] the deeds of the body, ye shall live" (8:13). Apart from the help of God, this kind of life would be impossible to us. This is the outworking of the grace of God in us.

Consider once more a verse we have looked at several times. Romans 10:4 "For Christ means the end of our struggle for righteousness-by-the-law for everyone who believes in him." Any and all struggle to live righteously will end once we know the Holy Spirit. He will do for us what we cannot do for ourselves.

The "how" of this is stated in Galatians 5:6: "For in Jesus Christ neither circumcision availeth any thing, nor uncircumcision; but faith which worketh by love." The "how" is "faith which worketh by love." In contrast to this is self-effort which always ends in failure. Self-effort and unbelief go together, and when they are present they cut us off from the grace of God. This is how we fall from grace.

The Galatian believers who accepted the teaching of the Judaizers fell into this experience. Paul wrote to them, "Ye did run well; who did hinder you that ye should not obey the truth? This persuasion cometh not of him that calleth you. A little leaven leaveneth the whole lump" (Gal. 5:7-9). The Apostle said that these believers had been making good progress in the Christian life then something went wrong. They ceased to go forward with the Lord. Paul added that whoever had persuaded them to change their course of life did not receive their teaching from God.

There was a little leaven among the Galatian believers. Leaven always speaks of something sinful which spreads its evil influence. What had started out in a small way was adversely affecting the spiritual life of the whole church. It was causing Christians to fall from grace, thus cutting them off from the very thing they needed for Christian growth.

The Remedy

The remedy for this situation is very simple and very simply stated. It is found in Galatians 5:16: "Walk in the Spirit, and ye shall not fulfil the lust of the flesh." The same truth is given in other words in verse 25: "If we live in the Spirit, let us also walk in the Spirit." The secret of Christian victory, that is the secret of overcoming evil in the Christian's life, is to live under the control of the Holy Spirit each step of our walk. Our Saviour taught this same truth when He said, "Abide in me, and I in you. As the branch cannot bear fruit of itself, except it abide in the vine; no more can ye, except ye abide in me. I am the vine, ye are the branches: He that abideth in me, and I in him, the same bringeth forth much fruit: for without me ye can do nothing" (John 15:4,5).

Love is the fulfilling of the Law. And we have learned that faith works by love. This is all related to walking in the Spirit as these verses show us: "This I say then, Walk in the Spirit, and ye shall not fulfil the lust of the flesh. For the flesh lusteth against the Spirit, and the Spirit against the flesh: and these are contrary the one to the other: so that ye cannot do the things that ye would. But if ye be led of the Spirit, ye are not under the law" (Gal. 5:16-18).

CHAPTER THIRTEEN

THE SPIRIT AND THE FLESH

In every believer there is a conflict which is expressed graphically for us in Galatians 5:16-25.

"This I say then, Walk in the Spirit, and ye shall not fulfil the lust of the flesh. For the flesh lusteth against the Spirit, and the Spirit against the flesh: and these are contrary the one to the other: so that ye cannot do the things that ye would. But if ye be led of the Spirit, ye are not under the law. Now the works of the flesh are manifest, which are these; Adultery, fornication, uncleanness, lasciviousness, idolatry, witchcraft, hatred, variance, emulations, wrath, strife, seditions, heresies, envyings, murders, drunkenness, revellings, and such like: of the which I tell you before, as I have also told you in time past, that they which do such things shall not inherit the kingdom of God. But the fruit of the Spirit is love, joy, peace, longsuffering, gentleness, goodness, faith, meekness, temperance: against such there is no law. And they that are Christ's have crucified the flesh with the affections and lusts. If we live in the Spirit, let us also walk in the Spirit."

Here we have two contrasting elements in our lives, the flesh on the one side and the Holy Spirit on the other. These are in direct contrast to each other. They are two opposing sources from which expressions of conduct flow. If we live our own lives we express the flesh. If we live the Christ life it is because of the Holy Spirit within us. "The flesh" and "the Spirit" are the basic terms of our identification with the human family on the one hand, or with the divine family on the other. To live after the flesh is our identification with the human family with Adam as our forefather. If we live after the Spirit, that is our identification with the divine family which is born of God.

In Adam we all inherit "the flesh." In Christ, those who place their trust in Him, inherit the Holy Spirit. The flesh has its way of living or expressing itself which is just the very opposite of the way of the Holy Spirit expresses Himself. These two are in direct contrast to each other. The desires of the flesh are opposed to the desires of the Spirit, and the desires of the Spirit are opposed to the flesh. As long as this conflict is unresolved in us, we cannot do the things that we would.

This was the experience Paul told about in Romans 7. He said there were things he wanted to do but could not. Then there were other things he did not want to do and he found himself doing them. This very condition led him under inspiration to give us God's analysis of what goes on in our hearts. The flesh, or the old nature, the fallen nature from Adam is in every believer as long as we dwell in these unredeemed bodies. It is not eradicated, even though some teachers have taught that it is. The Holy Spirit is also within us, for He has been given to every believer. The Spirit is there to subdue and conquer that flesh nature so that we can be free to do the will of God. Our choice in each instance decides whether we enjoy victory or defeat.

Remember, the teaching given here in Galatians 5 and Romans 7 and other portions dealing with this same truth is concerned with believers. An unbeliever has a flesh nature but not the Holy Spirit. The Christian has both the flesh nature and the Holy Spirit dwelling within Him.

Victory Not by Self-effort

A mistake made by many of us Christians is that we try to gain victory over the flesh by our own will and efforts. But this is the same as pitting the flesh against the flesh. We are trying to overcome the flesh by using the flesh. We might as well assign the Devil the task of conquering the Devil. Yet our Saviour was accused of this very thing during His public ministry. We learn from Matthew 12 beginning with verse 24: "But when the Pharisees heard it, they said, This fellow doth not cast out devils, but by Beelzebub the prince of the devils. And Jesus knew their thoughts, and said . . . And if Satan cast out Satan, he is divided against himself; how shall then his kingdom stand?" It is impossible to overcome the flesh by the flesh.

The flesh and the Holy Spirit are contrary one to the other. Their aims and purposes are diametrically opposed to each other. Each one says No to the other. They checkmate each other. This, of course, results in a stalemate for the Christian. This is why the Apostle says, "Ye cannot do the things that ye would."

What is the solution to this problem? In one sense the Christian has a more difficult time than the unsaved person, for the unsaved do not have the spiritual conflict in their hearts caused by the presence of the Holy Spirit when the flesh wants to do wrong. Usually the unbeliever just goes ahead and does as the flesh nature desires. There is nothing to hold him back. But when the Christian wants to do evil, the Holy Spirit is there to check the wrong tendencies and to direct the Christian into the pathway of obedience to the Lord.

Decide to Walk in the Spirit

Someone has given the following as a solution to this problem: "The Lord has voted for me, the Devil has voted against me, whichever way I vote, so goes the election." If we determine to walk in the Spirit, we are casting our vote in the right way. This is the choice we must make if we are to overcome the lust of the flesh.

The way of deliverance, then, is to walk in the Spirit (v. 16). We are to be led by the Spirit (v. 18). And we are to live in the Spirit (v. 25). If we give the Holy Spirit a free hand, if we let our lives be the practical day-by-day expression of His life in us, we will be victors.

The fact that there is this conflict is the reason for the subject under consideration often being called "the Christian's warfare." It began back in Genesis. When man was created he was created a living soul. He was provided with a mind which someone has called "the calculator;" he was given emotions which someone has called "the reactor;" and

he also had the will which has been called "the executor."
It is right here where the conflict lies. In the Christian both
the flesh and the Spirit seek to control the mind and the
emotions and the will. Do we think according to the Spirit
or according to the flesh? Are our emotional reactions according to the Spirit or the flesh? Are our decisions according to
the flesh or the Spirit?

The mind is where we do our planning. Our emotions
are the basis of our reactions. With our will we make our
decisions. So whether the flesh or the Spirit is in control
is up to us. It is our responsibility to choose to let the Spirit
direct us.

The Flesh Defined

It might be well at this time to define what the flesh is.
In a context such as Galatians 5 the word "flesh" is not
describing the body even though the body is made up of
flesh and blood. Neither is the Apostle speaking of our personality. The body in itself is not evil. The personality in
itself is not bad either. It is when the personality decides in
favor of the flesh that the personality is characterized by evil
and the body is used to express evil actions. The flesh is the
seat of sin within a man. It is the sinful element in man's
nature which he received from fallen Adam. It is the result
of the infiltration of the Enemy into the human race.

Familiar to most of us is the story of the Trojan horse.
The Greeks had laid siege to Troy for a long time and decided
to resort to strategy in order to take it. They built a large
wooden horse just outside the walls of Troy, and then left as
though they had abandoned the siege. The Trojans thinking
this was the case and finding the wooden horse, took it into
their city, believing they had won the victory. But during the
night while the people slept, the Greek soldiers who had
been hiding in the wooden horse came out of it and opened
the city gates to the Greek army which had returned under
the cover of darkness.

In my thinking I liken the flesh to the Trojan horse. It
is the flesh which opens the gate so that the forces of the

enemy can invade our souls. This is the strategy of Communism as it infiltrates governments and cultures and works from within to destroy peoples' freedoms. This is also the way of the flesh. It works from within to control us, every part of us—body, personality, mind, emotions and will. It is the old corrupt self that shows its true character when a man is left to himself. It is human nature which has been corrupted through the entrance of sin. It is man as he is apart from Jesus Christ and the Holy Spirit. The flesh is a fallen sinful nature that indwells each one of us.

Man tries to educate this nature. He tries to make it think good thoughts. This is the basic idea behind some of our present-day religions. "If we think good thoughts we will perform good actions." But this is like trying to train or educate the old nature to do good when its character is to do evil.

Discipline of a sort is also tried. They tell us to use our will power. Even laws are passed to make this old nature of ours behave. A certain amount of control is possible, but the anarchy becoming rampant today is a clear indication of what man really is on the inside.

God condemns unsparingly the flesh nature. He tells us that it is incurably bad. It cannot be educated or trained or disciplined to change its character. It refuses to be subject to the law of God. Paul learned to have no confidence in the flesh (Phil. 3:3). He confessed in Romans 7:18 that in him, in his flesh, dwelt no good thing. He went on to say, "For to will is present with me; but how to perform that which is good I find not" (Rom. 7:18). Where did he get the will to do good? That came from the presence of the Holy Spirit within him. The flesh never wants what is good, only what is evil.

Whether we were raised in a fine Christian family or came from a home that disregarded Christian things entirely, the flesh in us is corrupt and incurably bad. There is nothing good in it.

The Law Cannot Control the Flesh

God tells us in Galatians 5:18 that if we are led of the Spirit we are not under the Law. This means that no law can be found that will control the old flesh. This also means that victory over the flesh is not possible through the Law. As we have seen, verse 16 provides the solution for victory: "This I say then, Walk in the Spirit, and ye shall not fulfil the lust of the flesh." False teachers had come to Galatia stating that without the restraint of the Law the Christians would fall into sin. The very opposite was the case. They needed the Spirit of God, not the Law to provide both the motivation for good and a life of righteousness.

Even today some preachers in churches considered gospel churches, object to this teaching concerning the Law. They believe that unless they hold the axe of the Law over people's heads these folks will lose their salvation.

Paul, directed of God, declares that this is not so. It is only as believers govern their lives by the inward impulses of the Holy Spirit that He takes over the responsibility to see that we do not fulfill the lusts of the flesh.

A Life Conformed to the Holy Spirit

We are to walk in the Spirit, which means we are to order our manner of life or behavior in conformity with the Holy Spirit. The Law can hold up the standard of righteousness but it cannot empower us to fulfill that standard. Only the Spirit can do this. The responsibility to walk, however, is ours. When Daniel was confronted with being defiled through eating the king's food, he determined within himself that he would not give in to such a practice. He had to make that decision for himself. No one else could do that for him. This is the responsibility we, too, have to meet.

Every step of the way we must walk after the Spirit. And the way we walk is one step at a time. The Spirit has taken up His permanent residence in every believer. He is present to minister to the spiritual need of each person who trusts in Christ. The result is: "For what the law could not do, in that it was weak through the flesh, God sending his own Son in the likeness of sinful flesh, and for sin, condemned sin in the flesh: That the righteousness of the law might be fulfilled in us, who walk not after the flesh, but after the Spirit" (Rom. 8:3,4).

The word "lust" refers to the strong desires, the impulses and the passions, and in this case they are all evil ones of the flesh. Now the power of this depraved nature was broken when the believer accepted Jesus Christ as his Saviour. But the Holy Spirit and our cooperation with Him, is necessary before sin's power is broken in reality in our lives.

The constant pull of the flesh is toward evil things just as smoke from a fire flies upward. The old nature or the old flesh is constantly gnawing at the believer, desiring to express itself, for it is not eradicated. But its power has been broken; and if we will give full control over to the Holy Spirit, the desires of the flesh and the actions of the flesh will not find their fulfillment in us. We may be tempted to sin but that is not necessarily sin. It is fulfilling the temptation that is sin.

The Method of Victory

The believer is put in the responsible place of refusing to obey the evil nature. Perhaps our experience has been like that of many others: we have tried often but have failed. But have we really fulfilled the requirements of walking after the Spirit? Have we given an emphatic No to the desires of the flesh, and an emphatic Yes to the Holy Spirit who is within?

Perhaps we have had the experience of driving along one of our nation's highways letting our minds fill up with a number of different things. Then we have found that in an unguarded moment an evil thought has entered our minds. Satan has shot one of his arrows at us. The shooting of the arrow is not something we are responsible for, however. We cannot help what has happened. But we are responsible for what happens after the thought comes.

The 6th chapter of Romans tells us how to handle the situation. There we are told that we have died to the old self-nature. In my own case, when such an event takes place, I say out loud: "I am dead to you." I have an emphatic No for the flesh nature. Then I turn to the Holy Spirit who lives within and say, "I am alive to You. I want You to take over." Remember what Galatians 2:20 tells us: "The life which I now live in the flesh I live by the faith of the Son of God, who loved me, and gave himself for me."

The late Professor Wuest in his book, *Galatians in the Greek New Testament* wrote: "The will of the person has been liberated from the enslavement to sin which it experienced before salvation, and is free now to choose the right and refuse the wrong. The Holy Spirit has been given him as the Agent to counteract the evil nature, but He does that for the saint when that saint puts himself under His control, and by an act of his free will, says a point-blank positive NO to sin. In other words, there must be a cooperation of the saint with the Holy Spirit in His work of sanctifying the life. The Holy Spirit is not a perpetual motion machine which operates automatically in the life of the believer. He is a divine Person waiting to be depended upon for His ministry, and expecting the saint to cooperate with Him in it. Thus the choice lies with the believer as to whether he is going to yield to the Holy Spirit or obey the evil nature. The Spirit is always there to give him victory over that nature as the saint says a point-blank NO to sin and at the same time trusts the Spirit to give him victory over it" (p. 154).*

The Amplified New Testament translates verse 17 in this way: "For the desires of the flesh are opposed to the (Holy) Spirit, and the [desires of the] Spirit are opposed to the flesh (Godless human nature); for these are antagonistic to each other—continually withstanding and in conflict with each other—so that you are not free but are prevented from doing what you desire to do" (Gal. 5:17). The King James puts it very briefly: "The flesh lusteth against the Spirit, and the Spirit against the flesh." Wuest translates: "For the flesh constantly has a strong desire to suppress the Spirit, and the

*Kenneth S. Wuest, *Galatians in the Greek New Testament* (Wm. B. Eerdmans Publishing Co.) Used by permission.

Spirit constantly has a strong desire to suppress the flesh. And these are entrenched in an attitude of mutual opposition to one another, so that you may not do the things that you desire to do" (p. 154).

Wuest's comments are as follows: "When the flesh presses hard upon the believer with its evil behests, the Holy Spirit is there to oppose the flesh and give the believer victory over it, in order that the believer will not obey the flesh, and thus sin. When the Holy Spirit places a course of conduct upon the heart of the believer, the flesh opposes the Spirit in an effort to prevent the believer from obeying the Spirit. The purpose of each is to prevent the believer from doing what the other moves him to do. The choice lies with the saint. He must develop the habit of keeping his eyes fixed on the Lord Jesus and his trust in the Holy Spirit. The more he says NO to sin, the easier it is to say NO, until it becomes a habit. The more he says YES to the Lord Jesus, the easier it is to say YES, until that becomes a habit.

"The will of the believer is absolutely free from the compelling power of the evil nature. If he obeys the latter, it is because he chooses to do so" (pp. 154,155).*

This then is what Paul means in verse 1 when he says, "Stand fast in the liberty wherewith Christ hath made us free." We have been freed from the enslavement of the old nature. We have been made free to choose which direction we want to go. If we follow the old nature it is because we choose to do so. If we follow the Spirit is is because we have chosen to follow in that direction. The conflict spoken of in verse 17 of this chapter in Galatians has been going on in us ever since we were born again. The result will depend on the way we decide to go.

Because the Galatian believers had turned from Christ, Paul was praying for them that Christ might be formed in them once more. They had set Him aside through trying to follow the Law as the way of life. They had failed because the factor of the Law had been allowed to enter. But now a

*Kenneth S. Wuest, *Galatians in the Greek New Testament* (Wm. B. Eerdmans Publishing Co.) Used by permission.

new opportunity was theirs inasmuch as the Spirit of God had entered to minister spiritual life to those who really wanted to walk with the Lord.

God's provision is such that man has been set free from the Law, free from the bondage of the evil nature, free to depend upon the Holy Spirit so that He can create the life of Christ within. So the admonition is to walk in the Spirit which means walking in the Spirit a step at a time. In this way we will not fulfill the lusts of the flesh. If we walk in the Spirit, we are led by the Spirit and the Law finds nothing in us to condemn.

The blessed freedom of the Spirit-led person is such that his moral and spiritual life are above the power and ability of the Law to censor, condemn, or punish. This is the true moral freedom which is presented for us so clearly in Romans 8. This remarkable chapter begins with the words: "There is therefore now no condemnation to them that are in Christ Jesus." The reason is that once a person is in Christ Jesus the Law cannot condemn him. The passage goes on to state that "the law of the Spirit of life in Christ Jesus [this is the new life principle] hath made me free from the law of sin and death. For what the law could not do, in that it was weak through the flesh, God sending his Son in the likeness of sinful flesh, and for sin, condemned sin in the flesh: That the righteousness of the law might be fulfilled in us, who walk not after the flesh, but after the Spirit."

To walk in the Spirit is to overcome the flesh. When temptation comes suddenly, and that is the way it usually comes, the old nature will prod us on, but we must give him an emphatic NO. Then let us turn to the Spirit and say an emphatic YES. Victory in Christ is as simple as that. Believe that the Spirit will take over. This is an attitude of faith. We live by faith. We can then wait with confidence for the righteousness which will be fulfilled in us through the Holy Spirit.

CHAPTER FOURTEEN

THE WORKS OF THE FLESH

Perhaps we wonder why there are degrees of wickedness in men. Some are so very wicked while others seem good by comparison. The fact is, we could all be exceedingly bad under certain circumstances and conditions. This holds true for the Christian as well as the unbeliever, because all of us have a fallen nature which is incurably wicked. This is not a pleasant subject; nevertheless we must reckon with it, for the potential to sin in the believer is as great as in any other person. This the Bible teaches and we believe the Bible.

The flesh nature in an unsaved person or in a Christian, in a good-living person as well as in an exceedingly wicked person, is exactly the same kind of nature. There is no difference between the flesh nature in the best man and the flesh nature in the worst man. The flesh has the same potentialities in each person.

We can thank God that in the Christian there is the indwelling Holy Spirit to give power to check and to suppress the activity of this old nature, the evil principle in all of us.

This is one of the great basic differences between the believer and the unbeliever. But the sad part is that too many Christians do not walk fully in the Spirit. This is why there is often so much bad among those who should be good.

Another factor to take into consideration is that not all persons will do all that the flesh is capable of doing. One man may steal and another murder. Another may do neither of these and yet lie or show wickedness in other directions. Yet we are all capable of going the limit, for the potentialities of fallen human nature are the same in all of us.

In the 5th chapter of Galatians the Apostle Paul lists the variety of ways in which the self-life expresses itself. The list begins with some of the basic sins of sex and passion and then goes on to name some of the more refined sins that are often overlooked in so-called polite society. Such lists also appear in Romans 1:26-32; II Timothy 3:1-7; and Mark 7: 20-23.

Beginning with verse 19 Paul says, "Now the works of the flesh are manifest, which are these." By "manifest" the Apostle means that these works are open or evident. They are in plain sight for everyone to see. He also calls them "works." These are active evils rather than passive evils. Your flesh nature and mine and the flesh nature of every individual in the world has the potential to commit all of these sins listed and more.

In order for us to benefit from this study we will have to remember that what is dealt with here has to do with the old Adamic nature each of us inherited from Adam. It is not yet eradicated in any of us, and it will not be until we leave this body of humiliation. It is from this nature that the suggestions to sin come. It wants to control our bodies through which to express its evil acts. The mind, the will and the emotions it wants to control; and it will do so unless we submit these to the control of the Holy Spirit. So we must remember the Apostle is not here describing the man away from God, or who may never have come to God; he is describing us and the flesh nature that resides in every believer.

Sex Sins

The first work of the flesh mentioned is adultery. This is a sex sin in marriage or during marriage. Fornication is the sex sin that is more inclusive and has reference to such acts in marriage or out of marriage.

Uncleanness is next mentioned and is a sin similar to the first two except that it is a sin of the mind. It has to do with sensual thoughts, impure thinking. Our minds are capable of all of these.

Next is lasciviousness which is a sin that goes beyond the regular sex sins and describes one who had acknowledged no restraint. He does not stop at anything. He has contempt for public opinion and shamelessly outrages public decency. This is becoming more and more common in our own country. We used to associate it more with primitive peoples degraded by heathenism, but our own civilization and culture is seeing it more frequently.

Religious Sins

Verse 20 begins another series. Named are: idolatry, witchcraft, hatred, variance, emulations, wrath, strife, seditions, heresies.

Idolatry is the worshipping of an idol or the god the idol may represent. Perhaps we have not been guilty of this; nevertheless, the potentiality or the capability of doing it is in our hearts. The self nature does not want to acknowledge God. It wants to have a god of its own.

Witchcraft is next mentioned; here again some of us might want to relegate this to heathen lands and pagan religions. But witchcraft is associated with the use of drugs harmful to the health and personality and morality of the user. Along with witchcraft goes sorcery and magic arts. It is no mere chance that in many religions heathen priests have recourse to drugs that stimulate visions and produce highly excitable states of mind. The Egyptian sorcerers and charmers at the time of Moses were able to perform certain miracles through the power of the Evil One. There is more of this going on today than perhaps some of us realize, especially with the illegitimate use of drugs.

Next to be named is "hatred." This is the very opposite of love. It is enmity and hostility in whatever form it may be manifested.

Variance follows and this is a reference to contentions, fighting, discord, quarreling and wrangling. This comes a little closer home to some of us. This even shows up in our churches and in our homes at times. This is part of the works of the flesh.

Strife and emulations refer to jealousy and unfriendly feelings excited by another's possession of good things. We can become unfriendly toward other persons for the one reason of not being able to afford what they have by way of material possessions. Perhaps we do not have their income and so are not able to live on the level they do. This is envy, the desire not so much to have what they have but to have the same things.

Wrath is another work of the flesh. This has reference to passionate outbursts of anger or hostile feelings. It has to do with loss of temper and similar evil reactions.

Strife, on the other hand, has to do with self-seeking. It is a selfishness which divides. This is a sin that can do great harm among God's people. There are times when individuals, in the name of Christ, actually divide the Body of Jesus Christ. All such activity is of the flesh.

Seditions are dissensions and divisions. The flesh is a great divider and trouble-maker.

Last in this section is the word "heresies." Heresies are seen in self-opinionated interpretations of Scripture which twist the Word of God. It is not true exposition. There is a great deal of this today.

Social Sins

The next group of sins mentioned is in verse 21: "envyings, murders, drunkenness, revelings and such like." Taken together they speak of feasting and drinking parties that continue on into the night. This is ungodly revelry, carousing, debauchery. This is not only the flesh as it dwells in others but as it dwells in us. We are capable of such things.

The Apostle goes on to say that those who do such things shall not inherit the kingdom of God. Here we must go to the original to get the meaning of the words "do such things." The thought here is of continuously practicing such things, or habitually practicing, so as to indicate the character of the individual, guilty of these things. God estimates a person's character not upon his infrequent action or an occasional failure here or there but upon his habitual actions. If a person continues to live and walk in the works of the flesh, that person demonstrates that he is not truly re-generated.

We have been emphasizing that this is the potential evil in every person whether born again or not born again. But we can be thankful that for the person born again there is the Holy Spirit who indwells him. The Spirit of God is able to suppress and hold down and keep from expression the deeds of the flesh.

CHAPTER FIFTEEN

THE FRUIT OF THE SPIRIT

The presence of the Holy Spirit within the believer produces positive good as well. We learn from Galatians 5:22,23: "The fruit of the Spirit is love, joy, peace, longsuffering, gentleness, goodness, faith, meekness, temperance: against such there is no law." The Holy Spirit produces His fruit in the life of the saint as that saint cooperates with Him in the work of sanctification. This is not a once-for-all work in our experience but something that continues on from day to day. It is through this that the indwelling Christ is expressed more and more in our outward actions.

The Little Word "But"

The small word "but" can show contrasts or remarkable negations. In this particular passage it makes a clean separation between the flesh and the Spirit. The contrast is as great as between light and darkness. There is no middle ground between the flesh and the Holy Spirit. It is either one or the other, not a combination of both.

There are many such uses of the word "but" in Scripture. There is the "but" of salvation in John 1:11-13: "He came unto his own, and his own received him not. *BUT* as many as received him, to them gave he power to become the sons of God." It is seen again in Romans 6:23: "The wages of sin is death; *BUT* the gift of God is eternal life through Jesus Christ our Lord." The same word marks the turning point with reference to condemnation: "Therefore by the deeds of the law there shall no flesh be justified in his sight: for by the law is the knowledge of sin. *BUT* now the righteousness of God without the law is manifested, being witnessed by the law and the prophets" (Rom. 3:20,21).

In Galatians 5 we see it as the "but" of sanctification. It marks the difference between the flesh and the Spirit. It highlights the contrast between trying to make the flesh behave with that of allowing the Holy Spirit His full freedom to do His work. Such is the teaching of verses 17,18: "For the flesh lusteth against the Spirit, and the Spirit against the flesh: and these are contrary the one to the other: so that ye cannot do the things that ye would. *BUT* if ye be led of the Spirit, ye are not under the law."

If ye are genuinely born of God there is a clear-cut "but" between the former life and the present one. We may not be all we should be, but we are not what we once were. We read in II Corinthians 5:17: "If any man be in Christ, he is a new creature: old things are passed away; behold, all things are become new." The old ways of the flesh can be subdued and crushed and in their place the fruit of the Spirit can be seen.

A Cluster of Fruit

The Scriptures do not speak of the fruits of the Spirit but the fruit—singular. So what we have before us is a cluster. Just as some fruits grow on trees in clusters, so the fruit of the Spirit is regarded as a cluster of spiritual fruit. They blend into one, producing whole Christian character. The works of the flesh, on the other hand, are many and spread sorrow and confusion.

In order to produce the fruit of the Spirit we must walk in the Spirit. The life we now live in the flesh body we live by the faithfulness of the Son of God who loved us and gave Himself for us. We recall that our Saviour reminded us to abide in Him and He would be abiding in us. He told us that the branch cannot bear fruit of itself except it abide in the vine, so neither can we unless we abide in Christ. Then He went on to say: "I am the vine, ye are the branches: He that abideth in me, and I in him, the same bringeth forth much fruit: for without me ye can do nothing."

To abide in Christ is to have no known sin unjudged and unconfessed. When the sin comes to our mind we must confess it. We must not follow our own plans and invite the Lord to sit in and approve them. We must find out what His plan is for our life. It must be a life in which He can share; in fact in which He has control. We dare not try to keep things for ourselves that are displeasing to Him.

At the same time abiding simply means to take all our burdens to Him. We get all our wisdom from Him, all our privileges and rights, and all our strength. It does not mean that we have to have an unceasing sense or consciousness of His presence. It is not that we must remember all the time that He is present. Our heart beats regularly and we breathe regularly but how often do we think of these things. There are times when we are conscious of them just as there are times when we become conscious of His presence. This is especially true when we start to think about Him. But we must ever carry an inner attitude of letting Him have His own way in our lives. This is what we mean by abiding.

The fruit of the Spirit, which is the Holy Spirit producing Christ in us, is the result of what we may call "a Christ-flavored fruit." To lack the quality of love, joy, peace and these other graces is to sin against the Holy Spirit. If these are not present in our lives, we are defeating His declared purpose in coming into our hearts to live and dwell and produce Christ in us. When we do not allow Him to do this, we quench the Spirit.

We read in Galatians 5:25: "If we live in the Spirit." This means "if we have become alive in Christ, if He has given us new life," then "let us also walk in the Spirit." We are to allow Him to work out His will in us. The Christian derives his spiritual life from the indwelling Spirit. This is the motivating power within us that produces the fruit of the Spirit. So then, if the Spirit of God is in us, He will produce this fruit so that it will become evident.

There are three aspects to this fruit, the first of which characterizes the inner man. This is evidenced by love, joy and peace. The character of expression toward other people is in longsuffering, gentleness and goodness. Then, in our character of expression toward God there is faith, meekness and temperance. In another place the Bible says, "Now abideth faith, hope and love, but the greatest of these is love."

Love—Character of Inner Man

It is no wonder that the cluster of fruit should begin with love for love is the motivating power within us. The reason for this is simple according to I John 4:8: "He that loveth not knoweth not God; for God is love." Then in verse 16 of the same chapter we learn: "And we have known and believed the love that God hath to us. God is love; and he that dwelleth in love dwelleth in God, and God in him." Love is the bond of perfection.

In our English language we have only one word for love. This has to contain all that we mean in the variety of feelings that range from what is base to the highest God-given love. The Greek language, in which our New Testament was written, was not impoverished in this respect. It uses several different words to describe love in its various aspects. It is essential that we find out which one of these words Paul uses when he says, "The fruit of the Spirit is love."

First of all, there is the word "eros" which speaks of love between the sexes. It is the love of a man for a maid. This word is not used in the New Testament, however, for by the time the New Testament was written, the word "eros" had come to mean "lust."

A second word is "philia" which describes the highest kind of human love. This word is used in the New Testament many times.

Strong Word for Love

The word the Apostle uses in this passage in Galatians is the strong word for love in the New Testament and speaks of God's love. It is the word "agape," and is used in the New Testament to express ideas entirely unknown to the secular world. It describes a new quality of love, a new attitude toward others and is born only within the Christian. It is impossible to have this love without the indwelling Holy Spirit. It is not a love any man can produce in Himself.

The word is used to mean undefeatable good will

toward all men. It is always an outgoing love. It is not a love that looks within or to feeling. It never seeks anything for itself. It does not matter how the individual may be treated, if he has this love in him he will not be resentful or antagonistic. He will always seek the highest good even of the person misusing him. Its chief ingredient is self-sacrifice for the benefit of the one loved. No better illustration of this can be found in the Scriptures than John 3:16: "For God so loved the world, that he gave his only begotten Son, that whosoever believeth in him should not perish, but have everlasting life." Then, of course, there is the great love chapter, I Corinthians 13.

The love we speak of here is different from ordinary human love. There is a definite emotional quality in human (philia) love, but "agape" love is Christian love without emotions in the sense we usually mean. It is an exercise of the will and of the mind. It is not the response of our feelings but a determination on our part to do something about a person in need.

With regard to human love we just cannot make ourselves love certain people. Some persons rub us the wrong way, yet we can love them with "agape" love. So one of the remarkable aspects of this kind of love is the ability and power and determination to love people we ordinarily do not like.

The expression of such a love is not automatic. It is the result or a victory won over the self-life. It is quite impossible to manifest this love without the special power of the indwelling Christ. There is a great deal of talk in many puplits about accepting the Sermon on the Mount and the need of manifest love. But no worldly man, no unsaved person can express Christian love. It can be expressed through the child of God only because the Spirit of God has shed abroad the love of God in the hearts of believers (Rom. 5:5). Christ who is God, is, as to His nature, love. He indwells us so that He might love in us and through us. It is this love that is the fruit of the Spirit. The Lord Jesus promised, "He [the Holy Spirit] shall take of mine, and shall show it unto you."

There is no point in commanding fellow Christians to love certain persons with human (phileo) love. The feelings and emotions of even God's children just will not respond toward certain individuals. Yet we are commanded by our Lord to love one another. This was one of His final admonitions. Of course, He was speaking of love (agape) that has its source in God.

I have a preacher friend whom I have known for all the years we have been in Nebraska. Another preacher began to give him a great deal of trouble, telling lies about him, doing everything possible to hurt him. My friend said to me one day, "I am going to love that man and win him by love." He did just that. He showered love on him, doing things for him, saying good things about him, even providing him opportunity to preach in places that would not ordinarily have been open to him. That is the kind of love we are talking about here. Only a Christian can love in that way.

This is not an easy truth for some of us to accept. Some Christians can hardly believe that the Lord teaches us we are to love our enemies, even those who slander us.

It was just as He was about to be betrayed and later crucified that our Lord laid down the principle by which He lived and by which He wants us to live. He said, "A new commandment I give unto you, That ye love one another; as I have loved you, that ye also love one another" (John 13:34). We may have no feeling whatsoever of emotional kindness toward someone who has done us harm, but we must set ourselves to love him in the sense the Lord speaks of here. We must determine in our heart and soul that we are going to do that person good. Such love is the fruit of the Spirit, and He can and will produce such fruit in us. This was part of what Paul had in mind when he stated in Romans 8:39 that nothing could separate us from the love of God. Nothing can alter God's determination to do good to those who do not deserve it, that they might be saved. And when we put our faith in Him, this love conquers. It will never be relaxed toward us.

Loved by God to the End

Just previous to this in Romans 8, the question is asked: "Who shall separate us from the love of Christ? shall tribulation, or distress, or persecution, or famine, or nakedness, or peril, or sword?" (v. 35). Are these things of such a nature that they will come between us and the love of Christ? Of course not! In all these things we are more than conquerors through Him who loved us. God will let nothing stand between Him and His purpose to do His very best for us.

God loved us so that He gave His Son for us, and therefore will love us unto the end. His determination to do the highest good on our behalf cannot be changed. His very nature is love. It is this kind of love that is the fruit of the Spirit and is shed abroad in our hearts by the Holy Spirit and produced as He forms Christ in us. Do we ever wonder what good Christ saw in us? The fact is, that He did not see anything good in us. He did not love us for the good in us. The record is: "While we were yet sinners, Christ died for us." But His love is expressed in even stronger terms: "For if, when we were enemies, we were reconciled to God by the death of his Son, much more, being reconciled, we shall be saved by his life" (Rom. 5:10). The love of Christ is not to be explained. It is something to be wondered at. Let us not forget however, that this is the love we now possess through salvation in Christ.

In his prayer in the Book of Ephesians, chapter 3, Paul pleaded: "That he would grant you, according to the riches of his glory, to be strengthened with might by his Spirit in the inner man" (v. 16). The purpose for this is that we might love as we should: "That Christ may dwell in your hearts by faith; that ye, being rooted and grounded in love, May be able to comprehend with all saints what is the breadth, and length, and depth, and height; And to know the love of Christ, which passeth knowledge, that ye might be filled with all the fulness of God" (Eph. 3:17-19).

In answer to such prayers as this God is going to work miracles in us so that we may be surprised how we will love unlovable persons. The person may be dishonest, hard to get along with, one who does us evil; but we will love him just the same. This, as we have pointed out, is through cooperation with the Holy Spirit. Such love is not a pushbutton affair. We must commit ourselves to the Lord and say something like the following: "Lord, I cannot love that person except as You love through me. I commit myself to You with the determination that I will express such love, but it will have to come from You through me."

The love of Christ which is placed in our hearts by the indwelling Holy Spirit is the controlling dynamic of the Christian life. It is this love that controls us as Paul states in II Corinthians 5:14: "For the love of Christ constraineth us; because we thus judge, that if one died for all, then were all dead: And that he died for all, that they which live should not henceforth live unto themselves, but unto him which died for them, and rose again."

The Christian is not hounded to do good to somebody else by fear that God will punish him if he does not. This love of God when awakened within us will act. This is also the motivating force in Christian liberty. It is not law that directs us but love. When the love of Christ is perfected in His people, they will not be desiring to go back into sin. They will want to do that which pleases Him. This is what takes place in our hearts when the love of God constrains us.

It was this love that motivated Paul to say in one place: "If meat make my brother to offend, I will eat no flesh while the world standeth, lest I make my brother to offend" (I Cor. 8:13). The Apostle was willing to set aside his liberty in Christ for the sake of a weaker brother. Law could not make such a change in Paul's life but love could and did. It is this love that makes us sensitive to the feelings and needs of others. It gives us a new awareness of what is good and wholesome and produces an increasing abhorrence of sin.

Joy

The fruit of the Spirit is not only love, it is also joy. Joy and happiness are not necessarily the same. We may not always be happy over the way things are going, but we may still have the joy of the Lord in our hearts. According to I Thessalonians 5:16 we are told to "rejoice evermore." Some will of course object and say that this is impossible under some circumstances. But the Scripture insists that this is not impossible no matter how difficult the circumstances are.

Suppose we are discouraged by events around us. Who is it that is discouraged? Is it the Holy Spirit? Never! It is our feelings and our fears that have brought discouragement. We consult them instead of looking to the Holy Spirit. It is when we abide in Christ that the Spirit of God can produce His fruit—joy—in us.

Many years ago a great earthquake did considerable damage in San Francisco, California. Many buildings were wrecked by the quake and others through fire started by the earth tremors. In the midst of this great tragedy an elderly grandmother was observed sitting in her rocking chair on her front lawn and singing. A passerby asked her how she could be so happy when the earth was cracking up. Her reply was, "I'm rejoicing to see how my God can change things."

From the natural standpoint the Christian knows sorrow just as any other individual, but he has resources in the supernatural, one of which is joy. The Christian is a person who should be characterized by joy. Evidence to this effect is found in Paul's own experience and in his writing of the Book of Philippians. It is a book that expresses the joy of the Lord all the way through. Yet Paul wrote it from a dungeon cell. He said in one place: "Rejoice in the Lord alway: and again I say, Rejoice (4:4).

Peace

Peace is the third part of this cluster of spiritual fruit spoken of in Galatians 5. Peace with God comes to us through the blood of Jesus Christ. But we can also have the peace of God, for the Saviour promised: "Peace I leave with you, my peace I give unto you: not as the world giveth, give I unto you. Let not your heart be troubled, neither let it be afraid" (John 14:27).

In spite of all the turmoil in the world and the troubles which can affect us personally, we can have peace in our hearts. The reason is that we know Jesus Christ can take care of all things for us. He said that in this world we would have tribulation then added: "But be of good cheer; I have overcome the world (John 16:33).

We are often reluctant to accept such statements because we feel that we cannot get away from worrying about conditions around us and the problems that face us. But where is there a Scripture that gives us the right to worry? Where is there a Scripture that says the Holy Spirit worries? If we are going to worry, let us do it on a scriptural basis. Of course, there is none. Our hearts are not to be troubled. We are not to fret ourselves about evil doers or concerning circumstances. Our Saviour repeatedly told us not to be worried sick about things.

Peace Excludes Anxiety

What kind of peace did the Lord Jesus have? Was He ever ruffled? Was He ever discouraged or upset? Did He ever abide under the circumstances? Never! He had this peace that He has promised to give to us. On our part, it is a matter of appropriating it. When we face disturbing situations, let us go to Him in prayer and confess that we do not have peace in our hearts but we will accept His peace. Thank Him for His goodness and kindness. Then God will give us peace in spite of the problems and troubles we may be facing. We have gone through deep trials at times at the Broadcast. Sometimes these have been financial, and at other times of another nature, but God has always given us His peace when we have gone after it. We must ask for it and expect to receive it. Yes, more than that, accept it!

The psalmist has much comfort to offer. He wrote in Psalm 37: "Fret not thyself because of evil doers, neither be thou envious against the workers of iniquity" (v. 1). Later he says, "Rest in the Lord, and wait patiently for him: fret not thyself because of him who prospereth in his way, because of the man who bringeth wicked devices to pass" (v. 7). There is no cause for us to get upset over situations.

God's remedy for anxiety is stated in Philippians 4: 6,7. This is a portion to mark in our Bibles, then to memorize it and apply it. We are to appropriate its truth. The passage reads: "Be careful [anxious] for nothing; but in every thing by prayer and supplication with thanksgiving let your requests be made known unto God. And the peace of God, which passeth all understanding, shall keep your hearts and minds through Christ Jesus." We are not to be anxious about things, that is, we are not to worry about them. Our peace is not to be disturbed. There are natural tendencies in all of us to let certain things upset us. That may be one thing in your life and another thing in mine. God is interested in every detail of our lives, so He tells us that in everything by prayer and supplication with thanksgiving we are to make our requests known to Him.

Let us take a closer look at this passage. This is God's prescription for worry and when appropriated it brings peace. No matter what the event or circumstance, we are first of all to take everything to the Lord in prayer. This should need little if any comment. In the second place we are to approach God "by supplication." This deals with personal prayer, not mere general praying. These are to be very personal requests based on Scripture. Following this is a very important ingredient, namely thanksgiving. Our requests are to be made known to God with thanksgiving. So God places thanksgiving right alongside prayer and supplication.

A great many people have the habit of saying at the end of their prayer: "Father, we will be careful to thank you for this." If we are going to wait until we receive the answer before we thank God, we will very likely forget to thank Him. Let us thank Him before the answer comes. Then let us thank Him when it comes.

God wants us to make thanksgiving part of our prayer. We are to ask Him for what we need in explicit terms basing our claim on Scripture. This is supplication. We should thank Him right then and there for the answer.

Some will object by saying that they have not seen the answer yet, so why thank God?

We do not have to see the answer. Faith does not have to see, for faith accepts without seeing. There is the key to receiving the peace of God. I have found in my own experience that when I thank God for the answer to things I have asked for, peace comes into my heart. The answer may not be in evidence at the time I pray, but I believe God. The subject of the prayer may be a financial matter or a health matter or something else and the answer in the future, not the immediate present. But peace comes to the heart because we know that God is going to do as He promised. The peace comes from Him.

So we have here the true remedy for worry or prescription for genuine peace. The Spirit of God will work this in us. It is only when we fall away from God's grace that we worry. Grace is present with us constantly to minister peace to our heart.

These three parts of the cluster of fruit called the fruit of the Spirit have to do with the inward state of our hearts. They are the result of the Spirit-controlled life.

Need for Growth

So if we do not have love, joy or peace the reason is that the Spirit of God does not have control of our lives. These are completely "out of this world." They are not natural to man. They are known to the spiritual man only. We do not enter into perfection in all of these at once, but there is a gradual growth as we exercise faith in the Lord Jesus Christ. Then the Holy Spirit who is working in us develops them in our hearts. We grow as we learn to trust Him and obey Him.

Paul did not claim perfection in any of these areas. He wrote to the Philippians: "Not as though I had already attained, either were already perfect: but I follow after, if that I may apprehend that for which also I am apprehended of Christ Jesus. Brethren, I count not myself to have apprehended: but this one thing I do, forgetting those things which are behind, and reaching forth unto those things which are before, I press toward the mark for the prize of the high calling of God in Christ Jesus" (3:12-14).

He continues with the following words: "Let us therefore, as many as be perfect [mature], be thus minded: and if in anything ye be otherwise minded, God shall reveal even this unto you. Nevertheless, whereto we have already attained, let us walk by the same rule, let us mind the same thing" (vv. 15,16). So today we may have more love, joy and peace than we had yesterday. We must not let these slip but at the same time, though we cannot claim that we are already perfect, we can continue to grow in the knowledge of Christ.

This is in line with Colossians 2:6,7: "As ye have therefore received Christ Jesus the Lord, so walk ye in him: Rooted and built up in him, and stablished in the faith, as ye have been taught, abounding therein with thanksgiving." It takes time to get into the Word of God and to allow Him to work these things out in us. It is a moment-by-moment experience. Even the Apostle Paul had to learn this. He learned it as he went along in the Christian life. Writing from a dungeon cell in Rome he said, "But I rejoiced in the Lord greatly, that now at the last your care of me hath flourished again . . . Not that I speak in respect of want: for I have learned in whatsoever state I am, therewith to be content. I know both how to be abased, and I know how to abound: everywhere and in all things I am instructed both to be full and to be hungry, both to abound and to suffer need. I can do all things through Christ which strengtheneth me" (Phil. 4:10-13).

Peter speaks of growth in the things of Christ in the same manner. He said: "As newborn babes, desire the sincere milk of the word, that ye may grow thereby" (I Pet. 2:2). In his Second Letter he wrote: "But grow in grace, and in the knowledge of our Lord and Saviour Jesus Christ" (II Pet. 3:18). We are not to grow into grace but "in grace and knowledge."

CHAPTER SIXTEEN

MORE FRUIT OF THE SPIRIT

The Christian's Attitude Toward Others

The second cluster of three in the list of the fruit of the Spirit is concerned with the Christian's attitude and actions toward other human beings. These are longsuffering, gentleness and goodness. As with all the other aspects of the fruit, these will be in evidence in our lives only to the extent that we obey the Lord, surrendering to Him our goals and desires and allowing the Holy Spirit to bear His fruit in us.

Longsuffering

Longsuffering speaks of steadfastness of the soul under provocation. We may test ourselves in the following way. If we are quick-tempered or easily upset when something goes wrong, we are not longsuffering. If we flare up in anger when someone treats us in the wrong way, or have thoughts of revenge, then we are not showing steadfastness of soul under provocation. On the other hand, if we patiently endure, it is because the grace of God is working in our hearts.

Consider how our Saviour conducted Himself under extreme trial. Peter says of Him: "Who, when he was reviled, reviled not again; when he suffered, he threatened not; but committed himself to him that judgeth righteously: Who in his own self bare our sins in his own body on the tree, that we, being dead to sin, should live unto righteousness: by whose stripes ye were healed" (I Pet. 2:23,24). We can see from this that the Lord Jesus Christ is longsuffering. He indwells us and is our spiritual life so that longsuffering on our part should not be something foreign to us but normal because of the indwelling Christ.

153

We have said that these three divine graces are to be exhibited in our lives toward our fellow men. See from the following illustration how God treated men whose sins against Him were so grave as to have brought down immediate judgment.

In Exodus chapters 33 and 34 we have the record of one of the saddest incidents in Israel's history. They had Aaron make them a golden calf before which they danced and worshipped as they had learned to do from the heathen Egyptians. Moses prayed for them and this is what God said of His own character: "And the Lord descended in the cloud, and stood with him there, and proclaimed the name of the Lord. And the Lord passed by before him and proclaimed, The Lord, The Lord God, merciful and gracious, longsuffering, and abundant in goodness and truth, keeping mercy for thousands, forgiving iniquity and transgression and sin, and that will by no means clear the guilty" (Ex. 34:5-7). God would have been perfectly just in destroying these heathen worshippers in the midst of His people but He is longsuffering. Moses stood in the gap for them and God forgave them.

Each member of the Godhead is the same as each other member in attributes. All are longsuffering. The Holy Spirit who is forming Christ in us is longsuffering and will produce this in our lives as we surrender ourselves to Him. The Holy Spirit reveals His longsuffering when He tries to produce the same in us but finds so little response at times.

But someone is bound to say, "I get impatient." Yes, we get impatient but not Christ who indwells us! He is longsuffering.

The Bible says, "tribulation worketh patience," that is it helps produce patience. Tribulation does this by showing us our failures. Then in answer to faith that submits to the Lord, He works out patience in us. Consequently, if we do not want tribulation we should not ask God for patience. But if we want patience, we can rest assured God will work it in us through tribulation. There is no need for us to try to live patiently without God's help. We might as well confess our failure every time we fail and trust Him to produce patience in us. It is the Spirit's work to do this, and patience will increase as longsuffering increasingly characterizes our expression toward others.

This is pointed out by Paul according to Colossians 1:9-11: "For this cause we also, since the day we heard it, do not cease to pray for you, and to desire that ye might be filled with the knowledge of his will in all wisdom and spiritual understanding; That ye might walk worthy of the Lord unto all pleasing, being fruitful in every good work, and increasing in the knowledge of God; Strengthened with all might, according to his glorious power, unto all patience and longsuffering with joyfulness."

Gentleness

The second work is gentleness. This is an additional quality that should prevail in our lives and penetrate our whole nature. This will mellow us from all that is harsh and austere. In this connection the Apostle wrote in Ephesians 4:30-32: "And grieve not the holy Spirit of God, whereby ye are sealed unto the day of redemption. Let all bitterness, and wrath, and anger, and clamour, and evil speaking, be put away from you, with all malice: And be ye kind one to another, tenderhearted, forgiving one another, even as God for Christ's sake hath forgiven you."

How can these ideals be realized in our lives? How can we put away our sins such as bitterness and anger and malice? How in place of these can we manifest kindness and tenderheartedness? Only by allowing the Holy Spirit to form the life of Christ in us, this is done by trusting Him to produce the same qualities in us as are in Christ.

Why is there so much unkindness among Christians today? Is it not because so many of us are not allowing the Spirit to control us? We cater to the old flesh, to the self-life, and we are self-willed in our daily contacts.

To be gentle means to have a sweetness of temper that puts others at their ease. The gentle person shrinks from giving pain to others. When we are in the presence of others and things are not going right, do we seek to put them at their ease? Or are we the type of persons who make others wonder if they should even be around us?

Kindness is a characteristic of God. This is clearly presented in Romans 2: "And thinkest thou this, O man, that judgest them which do such things, and doest the same, that thou shalt escape the judgment of God? Or dispisest thou the riches of his goodness and forbearance and long-suffering; not knowing that the goodness of God leadeth thee to repentance?" (vv. 3,4). God's kindness is shown on all sides of us. He never treats us according to the way we deserve. This, then, is a characteristic that should grow in us as we allow the Holy Spirit to develop it in us. Christ indwells us for this purpose.

Goodness

The third word in the list before us is goodness. There is no goodness in man. Paul confessed, "In me (that is, in my flesh,) dwelleth no good thing" (Rom. 7:18). Our Lord made it very clear that if He were only man then He could not be called good. Someone called Him "good Master" and our Saviour replied: "Why callest thou me good? There is none good save one, and that is God." Our Lord was saying in effect that only God is good. If He, Christ, were merely man as some thought, then He could not be good. The word "good" as a characteristic applied only to Him because He was the God-man. This we must remember in thinking of ourselves. Goodness is not a part of our natural condition before our salvation. According to the Word of God there is none good, no not one.

The word "good" carries the idea of having quality of moral worth. This we can see in God. He will work this out in us as we submit ourselves to the Spirit of grace.

Attitude Toward God

The third group of three in this cluster of the fruit of the Spirit shows what we should be toward God. Faith, meekness and temperance are the three.

Faith or Faithfulness

In this passage in Galatians 5 the word "faith" means "faithfulness." It has special reference to the faithfulness or fidelity produced in the yielded Christian by the Holy Spirit.

God Is Faithful

Faithfulness begins with God, for He is faithful. We ourselves could never be faithful to Him but He is faithful and will work out that characteristic of His in us by Christ who lives in us.

The prophet wrote many years ago: "It is of the Lord's mercies that we are not consumed, because his compassions fail not. They are new every morning: great is thy faithfulness" (Lam. 3:22,23). The word faithfulness carries the meaning of reliability and trustworthiness. When we say someone is faithful we mean we can depend upon him.

The faithfulness of God is seen in various ways in the Scriptures as the following portions prove. When we as believers sin and confess our sin we can depend upon God to forgive us. I John 1:9 says, "If we confess our sins, he is faithful and just to forgive us our sins, and to cleanse us from all unrighteousness."

God is faithful to us when we are tested according to what Paul tells us in I Corinthians 10:13: "There hath no temptation taken you but such as is common to man: but God is faithful, who will not suffer you to be tempted above that ye are able; but will with the temptation also make a way to escape, that ye may be able to bear it." God knows our hearts and in His faithfulness He will not in any way allow us to be tested beyond our ability.

God is faithful to fulfill the promises He wants to work out through us. "Faithful is he that calleth you, who also will do it" is what Paul wrote to the Thessalonians (I Thess. 5:24). This means that when God calls us to perform a task, He is faithful to meet His obligations to us.

There is wonderful consolation in the truth expressed by Paul in II Timothy 2:13: "If we believe not, yet he abideth faithful: he cannot deny himself." If we fail God, will He then fail us? Indeed not! He cannot fail of His promise. This was one of the early lessons given to men: "God is not a man that he should lie; neither the son of man, that he should repent: hath he said, and shall he not do it? or hath he spoken, and shall he not make it good?" (Num. 23:19). This is our God and He is faithful.

Even when I come to a weak moment and fail Him, His promises are still true. I may be weak in faith but He abides faithful. It is true that we are to appropriate His promises by faith, but when we fail, we need to come to Him admitting our failure and appropriating His grace and promises for restoration and advance in the Christian life.

We can also depend on Him when it comes to meeting Him at the heavenly throne. The promise in Hebrews 10:23 reads: "Let us hold fast the profession of our faith without wavering; (for he is faithful that promised)." The context of this verse is an invitation for believers to come boldly into the presence of God by the way of the blood of Jesus Christ-- a new and living way. We are urged to come with a true heart full of assurance of faith, sprinkled from an evil conscience, holding fast the profession of faith without wavering. All of this is based on the premise that God who has made these promises is faithful. He will hear us. This is His assurance.

Sarah, the wife of Abraham, experienced God's faithfulness. This is what we are told in Hebrews 11:11: "Through faith also Sara herself received strength to conceive seed, and was delivered of a child when she was past age, because she judged him faithful who had promised." Sarah did not believe God at first but came to this position later. She was persuaded of God that He was faithful and would not go back on His promise. She trusted Him, and in due time she was delivered of a child as God had said she would be.

We can trust God's faithfulness in the midst of suffering. We may often wonder in the midst of trial or pain if we can stand up to such things any longer. When we face such circumstances, we do well to remember this promise: "Wherefore let them that suffer according to the will of God commit the keeping of their souls to him in well doing, as unto a faithful creator" (I Pet. 4:19). Our Saviour in the hour of His greatest suffering said to His Father: "Into thy hands I commit my spirit." He will not allow us to suffer beyond the point chosen by Him. He is faithful.

Christ Is Faithful

Faithfulness is a characteristic of Jesus Christ. He is described in Revelation 1 as the "faithful witness." He came as the Word to express to us the Father. He expresses the Father's love and will. He witnessed before His disciples and others of God's compassion and God's purposes; and the record of those incidents and events carry the same witness for us. Our Lord was a faithful witness.

He is also described as a faithful High Priest; "Wherefore in all things it behooved him to be made like unto his brethren, that he might be a merciful and faithful high priest in things pertaining to God, to make reconciliation for the sins of the people. For in that he himself hath suffered being tempted, he is able to succor them that are tempted" (Heb. 2:17,18). Our Lord who is the Eternal God became man, and living as man on earth He entered into our sufferings. He understands what we face and now represents us before God as our faithful High Priest.

He is faithful as our Advocate before the Father when we are guilty of sin. The Apostle John wrote concerning this: "My little children, these things write I unto you, that ye sin not. And if any man sin, we have an advocate with the Father, Jesus Christ the righteous" (I John 2:1,2).

Christ was also faithful to the Father. Hebrews 3:2 says: "Who was faithful to him that appointed him, as also Moses was faithful in all his house." The Lord Jesus Christ was faithful to the Father who appointed Him to the task of redeeming our souls. So the Son of God is also faithful, first to the Father and then to us in administering to us what the Father has promised.

Faithfulness as a Fruit of the Spirit

Faithfulness is a fruit of the Spirit. This is what God will produce in us as we allow the Holy Spirit to control us. God seeks faithful men as Paul indicates in I Corinthians 4:1,2: "Let a man so account of us, as of the ministers of Christ, and stewards of the mysteries of God. Moreover it is required in stewards, that a man be found faithful." If we find ourselves being unfaithful, let us turn to the Lord and ask His forgiveness and claim His promise to produce faithfulness in us.

We also learn that if we are faithful over little things, the Lord will give us greater things to be responsible for. To the faithful servant the Lord said, according to Luke 19:17: "Well, thou good servant: because thou hast been faithful in a very little, have thou authority over ten cities." The same thought is expressed in Matthew 25:21: "Well done, thou good and faithful servant: thou hast been faithful over a few things, I will make thee ruler over many things: enter thou into the joy of thy Lord."

God wants to produce the faithfulness of the Spirit in us and reward us with greater things for our obedience. God in His unselfish love wants to do everything for us that will be for our benefit. Thus we are called upon to be faithful and trustworthy both in our dealings with man and with God.

Paul testified of Timothy that he was a young man who had great concern for the people God entrusted to him. Paul found him to be faithful to his God-given tasks. The Apostle also instructs the church that the teachings which God has given are to be committed to faithful men. The Church as a whole should be characterized by trustworthiness and faithfulness. And such will be the result if spiritual leaders set the example by life and word. God's people are admonished to be faithful unto death; and to those who are, the Lord says, "I will give thee a crown of life" (Rev. 2:10).

Let us examine ourselves in the light of these things. Are we persons on whom others can rely? Can we be fully trusted? Can it be said of us that we are true to our work? Can God depend on us? Are we prompt in keeping promises and meeting obligations? Faithfulness is a fruit of the Spirit, not of the flesh. It is a God-given characteristic, so let us, under the control of the Spirit, develop it to the fullness in our lives by trusting Him for His indwelling presence.

Meekness

Consider now the word "meekness" as the fruit of the Spirit. Meekness is a spirit of humility, a refusal to let pride have the upper hand. Meekness gives no place for pride and self-seeking and is climaxed in voluntary self-abasement.

Christ thought nothing of His reputation but emptied Himself and became obedient even unto death. But His meekness did not carry the meaning so often attached to it in modern usage as spinelessness or spiritlessness. The attitude of the average person today is that we must show pride in ourselves and let everyone know our accomplishments. Someone told me at one time that if a person doesn't blow his own horn, no one else will do it for him. But this was not the answer of Christ. Neither should it be ours.

Meekness is the opposite of seeking a high place among men. It is the opposite of pride or arrogance. Moses is reputed to have been the meekest of men. This is the record of Numbers 12:3: "Now the man Moses was very meek, above all the men which were upon the face of the earth." There were many who had spoken against him but he had not retaliated. He was not spineless, however. He was a man who could be terribly angered in a righteous cause. Yet he was a man who was humble and submissive to God. There was nothing spiritless or anaemic about a man of Moses' leadership qualities that could lead such a difficult people as Moses led out of Egypt to eventual victory. He was a man who combined strength and meekness in proper proportions.

Our Saviour revealed His righteous anger when He drove the money changers out of the temple. Yet He was meek. How do we treat others when they oppose us? What is our attitude when we come across believers who have fallen into error? Only the Spirit of God can produce meekness under such circumstances—and in fact, under any circumstances.

Temperance

"Temperance," the last of the fruit given specific

mention, should now be considered. The word carries the idea of possessing power or strength, having mastery or possession of something, or self-control. An athlete, for example, who is out to win knows that he must be temperate or self-controlled with regard to eating, sleeping, exercising and such things (I Cor. 9:25).

The Christian then must be the master of his own desires and impulses. They must not control him but he them. Of course, we must recognize that the self-control spoken of here is a fruit of the Spirit, which does not infer that we ourselves produce this control. One of man's basic failures is his inability to exercise self-control. For the life to be characterized by it, one must walk in obedience to the Holy Spirit. He does not merely impose restraints on the self-life but takes over the believer's heart and directs him in the realms of money, pleasure, desires for fame or gain or whatever else may be included. This is not intended to be an exhaustive exposition of this word but merely to point in the direction that it leads us. Since it is part of the fruit of the Spirit, it must be produced through the Holy Spirit.

CHAPTER SEVENTEEN

VICTORY OVER THE FLESH NATURE

The Apostle closes this list concerning the fruit of the Spirit with these words: "Against such there is no law" (Gal. 5:23). The Old Testament Law could not produce such fruit. Neither is there a law that will regulate these qualities. Through the Holy Spirit we have been lifted out of the realm of law into the law of Christ. The Spirit of God works in us to produce these various qualities of spiritual fruit by forming Christ in us. The life of Christ now becomes our life through the operation of the Holy Spirit. This is realized in us when we are filled with the Spirit or, in other words, are under the control of the Spirit. It is then that we meet the righteous demands of the Law so that the Law cannot condemn us.

The Apostle carries the thought of our victory over the flesh nature a little farther in verse 24. The words are: "And they that are Christ's have crucified the flesh with the affections and lusts." In His crucifixion, Christ included my flesh life. This is the old self life. Christ not only died for my sins but included also the sin principle. This is true for each one of us who are believers; and some very practical truth flows from this fact.

We have often emphasized the first part of I John 1:9 but tend to overlook the last part. The complete verse is, "If we confess our sins, he is faithful and just to forgive us our sins, *and* to cleanse us from all unrighteousness." Christ not only died that we might be forgiven, but He also died that we might be cleansed from the contamination of sin in our daily lives. Romans 6:6 tells us that "our old man was crucified with Christ." It is this that makes possible our victory over the flesh from day to day.

We learn from Colossians 3:3 that we have died and our life is hid with Christ in God. Familiar to us now is Galatians 2:20 which tells us that we were crucified with Christ with the result that we are now crucified with Him.

We see then that Christ not only died for our sins but He included the affections and lusts, the disposition and cravings of the flesh nature. He took these to the cross with Him and was buried. In this then He buried our bad tempers, our passions, our tendencies to evil. This is not eradication of these things but the fact that the ground work for our deliverance from them was laid in His death and burial. This is true in our position before God, and it is available to us in our walk or daily conduct if we will appropriate it. So let us reckon on it (Rom. 6:11).

Salvation to us is a once-for-all act. We are not saved again and again. When Jesus died for my sins, He died for all of them once and for all. When I accepted Him as my Saviour, they were all forgiven and condemnation became a thing of the past. At the moment of receiving Him I also became spiritually alive. He became my life. This coming alive we speak of as the new birth. Birth is something that takes place only once for each of us. Then after the birth event comes the daily living. This is something that is constant.

By the death, burial and resurrection of Christ I have the privilege of now living the Christian life. The negative side of this is that I died so that the new life may be produced in me. And this producing of life in me is a continuous thing from day to day.

We mark the birth of a child by the time of the birth—the day, hour and minute. The child takes its first breath at birth but from then on it has to breathe every moment of the day. The heart has to beat and nourishment must be received periodically. Our spiritual life has this parallel in that the new birth is once for all, and then there is the continuous living that follows.

How then are we to live this life? The answer is given in

verse 25: "If we live in the Spirit, let us also walk in the Spirit." This means that if our life, that is, our new birth is by the Spirit of God, then let us walk in the sphere of His influence. We are to be controlled by Him constantly. We are to order our conduct by Him. Every step we take is to be under His direction. Birth is once for all but walking is a step at a time. If we fail to see this, we may try to do the best we can and in so doing will utterly fail. We must recognize this need of moment-by-moment living in the Spirit and look to the Spirit of God to provide life and direction. "This I say then, Walk in the Spirit, and ye shall not fulfill the lust of the flesh" (5:16).

Illustration From Israel's Experience

The nation of Israel provides an illustration of what happens in the lives of many Christians. They begin well but they do not always continue as they should. God took Israel out of Egypt once and for all. This was like a birth. He separated the nation from Egypt by the Red Sea and broke the power of the Egyptians by destroying their army and rulers in the sea. The people left in Egypt were in no condition to continue the pursuit of the Israelites and enslave them once again.

The next thing Israel needed to know was how to walk with God. For two years God patiently taught them in the desert how to walk with Him. Then at the end of that time He gave them the opportunity to choose whether they would walk His way or try their own. At Kadesh-barnea they chose to go their own way, refusing to go in to conquer Canaan in His might and power. They said they were not strong enough. It is true they were not strong enough in themselves. But God had not asked them to go in and conquer Canaan by themselves. He said He would conquer their enemies for them.

Neither can you or I conquer the evil things in our lives. We do not have the strength to do so. God has not left us, however, to our own devices. The Holy Spirit indwells us to conquer and to overcome the flesh life and to produce the life of Christ in us.

The sad story of Israel's defection is told in Joshua 5:6: "For the children of Israel walked forty years in the wilderness, till all the people that were men of war, which came out of Egypt, were consumed, because they obeyed not the voice of the Lord: unto whom the Lord sware that he would not shew them the land, which the Lord sware unto their fathers that he would give us, a land that floweth with milk and honey."

The basic sin on the part of these Israelites was their lack of faith. When they did not obey the voice of God, they showed unbelief. Instead of going from Kadesh-barnea into the land they went back into the desert. This was the ultimate consequence of their not trusting God. They wanted to go their own way, so God left them to themselves and by themselves they could not enter the land.

Cooperate With Spirit of God

We have the Holy Spirit to enable us to live the faith life. The Spirit of God constantly puts a check on the flesh nature. The flesh desires against the Spirit and the Spirit against the flesh. My old nature does not want the things of the Spirit, but the Spirit brings to our attention the things we should know and reminds us that He is with us to overcome the desires and passions of the flesh. But we have to cooperate with the Spirit of God by letting Him control us.

If we walk in the Spirit we will not fulfill the desires of the flesh. So by constant dependence on the Spirit to help us, our moment-by-moment walk will please God. We must form the habit of committing everything in our lives to the Lord. This is not something we can do once and for all. There should be an initial moment of surrender and then an attitude following this of constant surrender. Each step of the way brings us to a new place of understanding of the first decision we made to follow the Lord. So we must trust Him constantly, for the Christian life is a faith life.

We must ever remember that there are three stages to our salvation. The first stage is the past and that has to do with the removal of the penalty of sin. This took place when we trusted Christ as our Saviour. There is a future aspect which has to do with our removal or being taken from the presence of sin. This will take place in a moment, in the twinkling of an eye when we shall be ushered into His presence at His coming. There is also the present stage of our salvation which has to do with the power and dominion of the Holy Spirit over sin moment by moment. We do not permanently conquer the flesh nature in our daily lives and experiences through a once-for-all act. But we do have the promise and assurance of moment-by-moment victory over the evil nature.

According to Romans 6:11 we are to reckon ourselves to have died to sin, but to be alive to God. We are to reckon true in our daily experience what is already true in our position before God. Then we are admonished not to let sin reign in our mortal bodies. How can we keep the fallen nature from gaining control? The moment a temptation comes let us turn it over to the Holy Spirit, asking Him to take charge of our lives.

Temptations will come to us as long as we live. It is not wrong to be tempted. The wrong lies in yielding to temptation. This is why we are admonished not to yield our members, our bodies, when the flesh desires to control us. We are to say a flat NO to the flesh nature and YES to the Holy Spirit. We are to yield ourselves to the Spirit of God as instruments of righteousness to God.

Some of us are weak in some areas of sin and some in others. And natural sins keep creeping in, such as temper, and jealousy and other habits. When tempted to these things give the Holy Spirit control. There are times when He suddenly takes away all the cravings for some things such as drink and tobacco if we will let Him do it. There are other times when our battle against evil tendencies is a moment-by-moment affair. At first this conflict with our turning to the Lord for help may be quite laborious to us. Later it becomes a habit that seems almost spontaneous as we turn to Him for victory.

The concluding verse in the chapter is an exhortation: "Let us not be desirous of vain glory, provoking one another,

envying one another." These are additional works of the
flesh which we will avoid if we "walk in the Spirit."

CHAPTER EIGHTEEN

SOWING AND REAPING

The sixth chapter of the Book of Galatians provides us with some very practical lessons in applying the truths we have been learning. Of necessity we have had to consider in detail some of the works of the flesh, but now we can turn to the other side and see how the future is bright as we let God speak to our hearts.

A key thought in this chapter is in the words: "Whatsoever a man soweth, that shall he also reap" (v. 7). We do not live to ourselves. Our lives affect others. If the kind of life we live is selfish we not only rob ourselves but we rob others who should see in us something better by way of an example. If, on the other hand, we live unselfishly, live Holy Spirit controlled lives, we become spiritual persons and our Christian brethren will be benefited and encouraged by us.

One thing we must ever remember and that is the harvest is sure. Sowing and reaping are inseparably linked together. God created everything, and it was to reproduce after its kind. Nine times in Genesis 1 we read the phrase, "after its kind." This is an unalterable law of God.

The farmer expects to reap whatever he sows. He does not sow one thing and hope to reap something else. Yet in the moral and spiritual realms many seem to think that they can sow one kind of life and reap another. They sow to the flesh and hope they will reap in the Spirit. This is impossible.

Think of the eternal future. If we are materialistically minded and sow to material things, what spiritual reaping can we hope for? If we do not sow to the spiritual now, we will not reap to the spiritual in the end.

The same is true in raising our families. How do we

train our children? What are we sowing into their hearts and lives?

Abandoned Responsibility

There are many parents who have abandoned this responsibility and leave it to others to sow for them. Someone has said, "The father works one shift, the mother another, and the children are left to shift for themselves." We cannot hope to sow evil things and reap a good harvest.

The Lord gives us a concrete example in Luke 19 of one who tried to shelve his responsibility. He told the parable of the nobleman who went to a far country to receive a kingdom for himself and to return. Before he went he called his servants to him and gave each of them a pound. On his return he called the servants into his presence. Several of them had sowed and reaped and were rewarded. But one hid his pound and kept it laid up in a napkin. His excuse was, "I feared thee, because thou art an austere man; thou takest up that thou layedst not down, and reapest that thou didst not sow." The judgment on the unfaithful servant was that the one pound he had was taken from him. The principle was, "From him that hath not, even that he hath shall be taken away from him" (Luke 19:26). This man did not try to sow; consequently he did not reap. For this reason the very opportunity was removed from him.

We must realize that God has given us great opportunities to serve him today. If we do not use these opportunities, that is sow the seed now at hand, there will be no future reaping.

The Law of Increase

The Bible also teaches that there is a law of increase. We read in one of the parables in Mark 4:20: "And these are they which are sown in good ground; such as hear the word, and receive it, and bring forth fruit, some thirty fold, some sixty, and some an hundred." According to this principle we can expect to reap more than we sow. When what is sown is good, the harvest is a cause of rejoicing. When the sowing is evil, the consequences are fearful indeed.

The Prophet Hosea tells us that certain ones have sown to the wind and would reap the whirlwind (Hosea 8:7). James sets before us the sowing involved in sin. He says in 1:15: "When lust hath conceived, it bringeth forth sin: and sin, when it is finished, bringeth forth death." We cannot escape the reality of this. If we sow to lust we will reap sin. And sin pays the wages of death. If we sow to the flesh, we reap the works of the flesh, some of which are named for us in Galatians 5. If we sow to the Spirit, we reap life everlasting. This is not only speaking of the gift of life which we receive when we believe but includes also the life of the Holy Spirit who produces His fruit in us. He that soweth to his flesh shall of the flesh reap corruption; but he that soweth to the Spirit shall of the Spirit reap life everlasting" (5:8).

Reaping in Eternity

As we live to the Spirit, giving our bodies over to His control and everything else about us, we will reap things of heavenly value for eternity. For this reason among others, Paul says in Galatians 6:9: "Let us not be weary in well doing: for in due season we shall reap, if we faint not." Here the admonition is not to become weary, not to let up by reason of weariness or long waiting for the fulfillment of the Lord's promises. We do not see all the fruit of eternity at once; we will see it eventually. The conclusion of I Corinthians chapter 15 is one of triumph: "Therefore, my beloved brethren, be ye stedfast, unmoveable, always abounding in the work of the Lord, forasmuch as ye know that your labour is not in vain in the Lord" (v. 58). This assures us that whatever is done for the Lord is not useless and empty. It has eternal values.

James takes up the same theme when he says, "Be patient therefore, brethren, unto the coming of the Lord. Behold, the husbandman waiteth for the precious fruit of the earth, and hath long patience for it, until he receive the early and latter rain. Be ye also patient; stablish your hearts: for the coming of the Lord draweth nigh" (Jas. 5:7,8).

So we are admonished not to become weary in well doing. We do not always see the results of our labors but we can rest assured that there will be a harvest. And while we wait and walk with the Lord the fruit of the Spirit will be born in us and exhibited through us.

We are also admonished not to faint. A person under extreme heat or undue excitement may faint, but we are not to give up. In the *Amplified* we find it stated this way: "For in due time and at the appointed season we shall reap, if we do not loosen and relax our courage and faint." We are not to become exhausted. If we seek to do the work ourselves, of course, our own strength will not last long, and we will become exhausted. Self-effort brings on fainting. But work done in the strength of the Lord will go forward with vigor. Isaiah brings out this truth very clearly in a passage that has encouraged me many times when I thought I could not go on: "Hast thou not known? hast thou not heard, that the everlasting God, the Lord, the Creator of the ends of the earth, fainteth not, neither is weary? there is no searching of his understanding. He giveth power to the faint; and to them that have no might he increaseth strength. Even the youths shall faint and be weary, and the young men shall utterly fall: But they that wait upon the Lord shall renew their strength; they shall mount up with wings as eagles; they shall run, and not be weary; and they shall walk, and not faint" (Isa. 40:28-31).

What a wonderful promise this is. It is fulfilled in us when we let the Lord work through us and exchange our strength for His. Let us sow in righteousness and we will reap in righteousness, both in this life and particularly in the life to come.

Restoring a Straying Brother

The Apostle gives three illustrations of sowing and reaping in this chapter. These are very important to consider. The first is found in verse 1: "Brethren, if a man be overtaken in a fault, ye which are spiritual, restore such an one in the spirit of meekness; considering thyself, lest thou also be tempted." This is not speaking of a Christian brother who persists in sinning but one who has been overtaken by a fault. The Lord has made provision for such as we have already seen in I John 1:9: "If we confess our sins, he is faithful and just to forgive us our sins, and to cleanse us from all unrighteousness." Then there is the promise in I John 2:1 for Christians overtaken in fault: "My little children, these things write I unto you, that ye sin not. And if any man sin, we have an advocate with the Father, Jesus Christ the righteous."

God has provided a way for such persons to be restored to fellowship and to usefulness again, but we must cooperate with God in helping them.

Who is told to restore the person caught in a fault? "He that is spiritual" says the Apostle. Who would dare respond by claiming such spirituality? Certainly not one who thinks he is more spiritual than others because he has a higher standard of spiritual living. The spiritual man or woman is the one living in total dependence upon the Holy Spirit. There is a place for humility here in contrast to boastful pride. We know that without Christ's help we can do nothing. But if we abide in him we will bear much fruit. Paul said in Philippians 4:13 that we can do all things through Christ who strengthens us.

If you know the truth concerning the Spirit of God as it has been presented in these studies and are under the control of the Holy Spirit, you can restore a brother who has been caught in a fault. But it must be done in meekness and humility. There is no place here for criticism. The fruit of the Spirit is love; so the man who is spiritual will also be the man who expresses love in his daily contacts with others.

Who Is the Spiritual Man?

The non-spiritual man and the spiritual man are clearly illustrated for us in the Apostle Paul's experience. In the third chapter of Philippians he tells what he was before his conversion, and this illustrates the man after the flesh at his best.

He was born an Israelite of the tribe of Benjamin and called himself an Hebrew of the Hebrews. He was circumcised the eighth day according to the Law. He became a Pharisee, a strict observer of the Law. Concerning zeal he persecuted the Church. So far as the legal observances of his religion were concerned he was blameless. Before men this was a spotless record. But Paul came to see that this standard by which he was measuring did not fit God's standard. He saw that what he thought was spirituality was produced by the flesh. So he came to the place where he counted all these things but loss for the excellency of the knowledge of Jesus Christ. What Paul wanted above all else was to know Christ and the power of His resurrection. This made the new man a spiritual man.

Present Christ

The spirit of meekness, as we have noted, is essential in the restoring of one out of fellowship with God. We have nothing of ourselves that will help the other person. Christ is the answer to his problem and we must show what Christ is and has for the needy Christian.

A person called me on the telephone a number of times, asking for my help with regard to some spiritual situations. Not once but several times I was asked to repeat a certain statement so that this person could say that Mr. Epp said, "so and so." My reply was, "This is the heart of your problem. You are depending upon what I am saying instead of what God says. What I say means nothing unless I can point you to Jesus Christ. If I fail in this, I am not helping you. Until you look to Jesus Christ you will not find the help you need."

The man after the flesh will reveal himself by the way he treats a fellow believer who has failed at some point or other. He will measure the erring brother by the standards of the law or by some standards set up by man. Criticism will not help the conscience-stricken believer. We cannot hope to set people in the path of God if what we do is done in the spirit of criticism or antagonism. It must be in a spirit of meekness which means we must be under the control of the

Spirit of God. The man who is spiritual knows the grace of God and is, therefore, gracious in his conduct and conversation.

There needs to be a bit of toleration in our disposition for people who differ from us in some things. We are not suggesting here that we should have any tolerance for false teaching or for the spirit of apostasy. But we must be merciful, longsuffering, kind and forgiving in our attitude toward our brethren in the Lord who may have been overtaken in a fault. The most caustic and derogatory letters we receive are almost entirely from people who object to our teaching of salvation and the Christian walk being by grace through faith only. The Bible warns us that if we bite and devour one another, we must take heed that we are not consumed one of another.

Danger of a Fault-Finding Spirit

One of the perils of an advanced spiritual experience is a spirit of censureship. Since we have grown in grace we expect all other Christians to measure up to our standards. If they do not, we pass judgment on them. This is the very thing God says we are not to do.

If we find a brother who has been guilty of misconduct or guilty of some sin or fault, those of us who are responsive to the control of the Holy Spirit should seek to set that brother right. We should try to restore him to fellowship with the Lord and do this without any sense of superiority. It should all be done in gentleness, keeping an attentive eye upon ourselves in case we fall into the same fault. It is not ours to judge in such a case or to condemn but to restore. A fallen brother needs help, not criticism.

In writing to the Philippians Paul said: "Let nothing be done through strife or vainglory; but in lowliness of mind let each esteem other better than themselves. Look not every man on his own things, but every man also on the things of others" (2:3,4). The Lord Jesus Christ is pointed to as the one Person to follow in this case. Here again it is only as the Spirit of God controls us that this will be possible. The Apostle says, "Let this mind be in you, which was also in

Christ Jesus; Who, being in the form of God, thought it not robbery to be equal with God: But made himself of no reputation." We become very concerned about our reputations. Jesus made Himself of no reputation. He set it aside for the sake of restoring lost man to Himself. Now that He indwells believers He is seeking to do the same thing through us.

Let us put ourselves, for instance, in the shoes of the man who is fallen. How would we have acted under similar circumstances—if we could even know what his circumstances were? Very often we have no idea of what caused a particular person to fall into sin. So, in restoring him, we must remember our own weaknesses and our own possibility of falling. All that is needed for us to fall is to ignore the Holy Spirit, even in one moment of temptation. It is just as easy for us to fall as the person we have found in sin.

If we ignore the Holy Spirit in a moment of temptation we find ourselves in a fault. Then we have to come clean again with the Lord. This happens to all of us. It makes no difference how long we have been Christians or how good we are as Christians. So we dare not overlook this possibility.

Some Christian might retort: "What do you expect of someone like me if you, an older Christian and a preacher of the gospel, are not free from attack by the flesh nature in these things?" The answer is that the old nature in me is no better than the old nature in a Hottentot in Africa. The flesh will never be any better in any of us. We will have to live with it as long as we are on this earth. But we also have the Holy Spirit in us, and the more we learn about His grace and His operations in our hearts, the more gratefully will we respond to His control and power.

What should be our attitude toward brethren who we may only suspect have fallen into a sin? A verse God has used in my own heart on which to base my attitude is the following: "So you must stop forming any premature judgments, but wait until the Lord shall come again. For He will bring to light the secrets hidden in the dark, and will make known the motive of men's hearts and then shall proper praise be awarded each one" (I Cor. 4:5, Wms.). God knows the motives of each heart. He knows why certain things were done. We do not, so it is very necessary that we do not judge prematurely.

In this same connection the Apostle Paul says: "But why dost thou judge thy brother? or why dost thou set at nought thy brother? for we shall all stand before the judgment seat of Christ. . . . So then every one of us shall give account of himself to God. Let us not therefore judge one another any more: but judge this rather, that no man put a stumbling-block or an occasion to fall in his brother's way" (Rom. 14:10,12,13). Let us then withhold judgment in cases where we are not sure until Jesus comes. When we do find a believer caught in a fault, let us restore him in a spirit of meekness to a living fellowship with the Holy Spirit. If our own motives and attitudes are correct, the Holy Spirit will take over and guide the erring believer through the Word.

God knows our various dispositions. He knows our weaknesses and knows if we seek to walk with the Lord. He knows all our backgrounds and circumstances and will not allow us to be tempted or tested above that we are able but will provide a way of escape. So then, the evidence of spirituality in any believer is the willingness to restore a fallen Christian in the spirit of patience, kindness, forbearance, longsuffering, forgiveness and pity.

CHAPTER NINETEEN

MORE SOWING AND REAPING

Right after the explicit instructions concerning the restoration of a Christian overcome by sin we have another illustration of sowing and reaping. We also have a seeming contradiction. It is only seeming however, for in reality it teaches us some very precious lessons.

The words are: "Bear ye one another's burdens, and so fulfil the law of Christ. For if a man think himself to be something, when he is nothing, he deceiveth himself. But let every man prove his own work, and then shall he have rejoicing in himself alone, and not in another. For every man shall bear his own burden" (Gal. 6:2-5). To speak of bearing one another's burdens and then to say that every man shall bear his own burden appears on the surface to be a contradiction. This really is not the case. Two different words are used in the original language that are translated "burden" in this passage. The Bible describes several kinds of burdens and so to these two in this passage we will also consider another one.

Bearing Another's Burdens

The burden spoken of in verse 2 is a burden caused by circumstances. The first verse in this chapter admonishes the spiritual man to restore a brother caught in a fault. Instead of discouraging the guilty and burdened brother, the Christian counselor is to help sustain his spiritual life. We are to help bear the burdens of such a person. We are to put ourselves in his place and make his burdens part of our burden.

When we see Christians as a whole going in the direction being taken today, it hurts us. But do we feel the same hurt when it is a single individual who is out of fellowship with God? If it is our child or one close to us, it certainly does hurt. But the same spiritual burden bearing should be entered into by us whether the relationship of the person is close to us or there is no relationship whatsoever.

Fulfilling the Law of Christ

In thus bearing another's burdens we fulfill the law of Christ. This, as we have seen in previous studies, is not a law such as the law of Moses but is the expression of divine love as brought into the renewed heart by the Holy Spirit. He has shed this love abroad in us, so that we can follow the admonition that tells us we are to love one another (II John 5).

The law of Christ is not an exterior law as we have indicated but something produced in the heart. This is the truth given in Hebrews 10:16: "This is the covenant that I will make with them after those days, saith the Lord, I will put my laws into their hearts, and in their minds will I write them." This was prophetically written concerning Israel, but it is a reality in each of our hearts now who have come to Christ. Christ Himself indwells us so that love, divine love, outflows from us when we are controlled by the Holy Spirit. The love of God constrains us to do and be what we should. The Law demanded love but Christ's law is love. The reason is that God as to His nature is love. And since Christ dwells in us, this divine quality of life is also within us. The law of Christ, then, takes the place of the external law by fulfilling the righteousness of the law in us.

When the Holy Spirit is in control of our hearts, we will find some way to help a fellow believer in need. In Romans 15 the Apostle wrote: "We then that are strong ought to bear the infirmities of the weak, and not to please ourselves. Let everyone of us please his neighbor for his good to edification. For even Christ pleased not himself; but, as it is written, The reproaches of them that reproached thee fell on me" (vv. 1-3).

We stand in the place of bearing the burdens of many needy souls. We shall not live for ourselves alone when the Holy Spirit fills us. The out-flowing of love from us to others will be almost an automatic matter when we are yielded to the Spirit. So, bearing one another's burdens is not a legal obligation placed upon the Christian but the response of a heart motivated by the indwelling Christ.

It is in this way that we keep the "commandments" our Saviour left us. His commandment is that we love one another. This is not a legal injunction, but when obeyed it is the test and proof of the filling of the Holy Spirit and of His fruit-bearing in our lives.

Bearing One's Own Burdens

Over against this admonition to bear one another's burdens is the statement in Galatians 6:5: "For every man shall bear his own burden." This is another kind of burden, and Paul introduces the discussion of it with the word "for." This word refers to something preceding in the context. Verses 3 and 4 contain the information. There we read: "For if a man think himself to be something, when he is nothing, he deceiveth himself. But let every man prove his own work, and then shall he have rejoicing in himself alone, and not in another." The thought is that if a man thinks himself too important to help a weaker brother, there is something wrong with that man. He is not meeting his responsibility of service. To feel ourselves superior in such a case, we only deceive ourselves. Our lack of concern reveals our lack of grace and love, therefore a lack of the fruit of the Spirit.

An illustration of this comes from I John 3:16,17: "Hereby perceive we the love of God, because he laid down his life for us: and we ought to lay down our lives for the brethren. But whoso hath this world's good, and seeth his brother have need, and shutteth up his bowels of compassion from him, how dwelleth the love of God in him?" This is not only material goods that are in mind but spiritual needs as well. If we see a man who is a brother in Christ and spiritually lacking and we do nothing about it, how can the love of God be dwelling in us? This would contribute a disregard of our discipleship.

Verse 4 in Galatians 6 begins with the word "but." We have seen before how important this word is in many portions of the Bible. This portion is no exception. It introduces the contrast between the burden of verse 2 where the Apostle says, "Bear ye one another's burdens," which are burdens of sympathy, and in verse 5 where he says that each man is to "bear his own burdens." The burden in verse 5 deals with our responsibilities as Christians. The subject of personal work is raised here and is part of our task as members of the Body of Christ.

In such passages as I Corinthians 12:18, Romans 12: 3-8, we are told we are members of the Body of Christ and the function of members in a body is to work. The life of the body is His life. So each one of us who is a member of the Body of Christ has a responsibility and must bear it thus proving his own work. To the sinner the Lord Jesus said, "Come unto me, all ye that labour and are heavy laden, and I will give you rest." But to us he says, "Take my yoke upon you, and learn of me; . . . for my yoke is easy, and my burden is light." He wants us to bear our burden of responsibility to God and man.

The Lord says His burden is easy. The reason is that He indwells us and enables us to carry that burden as we should. Our responsibility is to yield to Him and if He wants to use our mouth to witness to another, then let Him use it. If it is our hands that are to work, we yield them to Him. So in the light of what Galatians 6:4 says. "But let every man prove his own work, and then shall he have rejoicing in himself alone, and not in another." the Apostle is pointing out that we will prove ourselves and test ourselves when we have responsibilities to meet. And in finding out where we have failed, we will be more inclined to show compassion to others. We must give a personal account of our failures to appropriate the life that gives us victory.

We not only must answer for what we do that is wrong but for the fact that we have not allowed Him to work out His grace in us. According to Romans 14:10 we shall all stand before the judgment seat of Christ to give account of ourselves to God. What we do in this body will come up for review and for reward where it is due.

But in order to gain such rewards we must carry the burden of sympathy for fellow believers as well as meeting our own responsibilities before the Lord.

Burdens Caused By Cares of Life

So far we have dealt with the two burdens spoken of in Galatians 6:1-5. The first is a burden of sympathy that is called forth from us as we see others in difficult circumstances. The second is a burden of personal responsibility for discipleship and service. A third burden I wish to consider but which not mentioned in Galatians 6 is a burden that all of us have at times, the burden caused by a heart loaded down with the cares of life. We are instructed in the Psalms: "Cast thy burden upon the Lord, and he shall sustain thee" (Ps. 55:22). Or as Peter tells us: "Casting all your care upon him; for he careth for you" (I Pet. 5:7). The Lord in the Sermon on the Mount tells us specifically what the usual burdens are that the average person carries. He said, "Therefore I say unto you, Take no thought for your life, what ye shall eat, or what ye shall drink; nor yet for your body, what ye shall put on. Is not the life more than meat, and the body more than raiment?" These among others are burdens we are to cast upon the Lord.

A verse to which I have referred hundreds of times in my Christian experience is Psalm 37:5: "Commit thy way unto the Lord; trust also in him; and he shall bring it to pass." This is a verse that seems to include all our burdens. Let us commit them all to Him and He will take care of us. When we stop to consider what we have in Christ for daily living, it should cause us to rejoice continually. We have the Spirit of God within us to produce the fruit of the Spirit. We also have the promise of God that if we commit our ways to Him, He will see that the purposes of life He has outlined for us will be accomplished. Faithful sowing on our part in these areas will bring results for time and eternity.

CHAPTER TWENTY

FELLOWSHIP IN RECEIVING AND GIVING

The third illustration of sowing and reaping in Galatians 6 is found in verse 6: "Let him that is taught in the word communicate unto him that teacheth in all good things." This is a very touchy subject to some people. Yet it demonstrates whether we are walking after the flesh or after the Spirit. The subject is Christian stewardship or giving. To the person whose heart and life are totally committed to the Holy Spirit the subject of giving is not a touchy matter. Our response to the will of God is the response of love and to share financially in the work of the Lord is not burdensome. The love that God had for us in sending Christ to die for us is the kind of love that wants to see the other person benefited in every way possible. So with this kind of love in us since both Christ and the Holy Spirit indwell us, the subject of giving will not be a touchy matter. It will become a matter of joy.

The Bible speaks of Christian giving as a grace. This is something in which the Christian is to grow (II Cor. 8:7).

The key to where to give is found in the 6th verse where we are told that him who is taught in the Word is to communicate to him who teaches. A pastor asked me one day what answer should be given to a husband and wife who were wondering where they should give their money for the Lord's work. I pointed out this verse and said on the basis of the Word of God that Christians should communicate, in other words, give their gifts first of all to the source from which they are receiving spiritual blessing. So this means that the person who receives instruction in the Word is to share good things with his teacher. He is to contribute to that teacher's support.

The word "communicate" means "share" in this connection. The man who receives spiritual help is to provide material help in return. If I need a pair of shoes I go to a shoe store with money for that purpose. The man who has the shoes that I want wants my money. So we exchange values. This is what is expressed here, a sharing of values. This is a matter of sharing those things which God has already shared with us. This is the principle of giving that God lays down in this passage.

Paul stated this principle in I Corinthians 9 beginning with verse 11: "If we have sown unto you spiritual things, is it a great thing if we shall reap your carnal things? If others be partakers of this power over you, are not we rather? Nevertheless we have not used this power; but suffer all things, lest we should hinder the gospel of Christ" (vv. 11,12). Paul had led these Corinthians to salvation in the Lord; and for that reason and for the fact that he taught them how to grow in grace and to serve the Lord they had an obligation to him. Nevertheless it was one that Paul had not pressed. He did not receive their financial help. In fact, he did not expect anything from them, for he wanted the gospel message to go forth unhindered in their midst. However, the Apostle makes it very plain that what he did at Corinth was not the usual method followed. God's principle of giving is this: "Do ye not know that they which minister about holy things live of the things of the temple? and they which wait at the altar are partakers with the altar?" (I Cor. 9:13). The Apostle clinches his point in the next verse where he says, "Even so hath the Lord ordained that they which preach the gospel should live of the gospel" (v. 14).

In his Second Letter to the Corinthians the Apostle again takes up the subject of giving to those who teach us the Scriptures. In verse 6 of chapter 9 he says, "But this I say, He which soweth sparingly shall reap also sparingly; and he which soweth bountifully shall reap also bountifully." Since this is emphasizing supporting those who teach the

Scriptures it would include a work such as this that daily ministers Bible truth. This should not be done, however, to the exclusion of the local church if the pastor is feeding his people on the Word of God. In fact, in that case, that should be one's first consideration.

How Much to Give

The spirit in which believers give is dealt with next by the Apostle. This is the standard: "Every man according as he purposeth in his heart, so let him give; not grudgingly, or of necessity: for God loveth a cheerful giver" (v. 7). Following this is one which gives great encouragement to the believer and one I have personally learned to love: "And God is able to make all grace abound toward you; that ye, always having all sufficiency in all things, may abound to every good work" (v. 8). This is God's special promise to all who abound in the grace of giving.

On this same theme is a portion in the Book of Proverbs. The words are, "There is that scattereth, and yet increaseth; and there is that withholdeth more than is meet, but it tendeth to poverty. The liberal soul shall be made fat: and he that watereth shall be watered also himself" (11:24,25). I have myself practiced this and can assure you from personal experience that it works. It is a God-given principle that never fails.

The Apostle Paul tells in the Book of Philippians of an instance in which he was in great financial distress and the believers in Philippi came to his relief. He wrote to them: "Notwithstanding ye have well done, that ye did communicate with my affliction. Now ye Philippians know also, that in the beginning of the gospel, when I departed from Macedonia, no church communicated with me as concerning giving and receiving, but ye only" (Phil. 4:14,15). Then he added: "For even in Thessalonica ye sent once and again unto my necessity. Not because I desire a gift: but I desire fruit that may abound to your account" (vv. 16,17). This is our position at Back to the Bible. We want only for God's work here that which God has designated for this work.

Qualified Promise

Then follows a promise that many of us have quoted, but we do not always remember that there are qualifications to it. If we are obedient with regard to our gifts, the promise is for us: "But my God shall supply all your need according to his riches in glory by Christ Jesus" (Phil. 4:19). If we sow, God will supply our need. By sowing in obedience to Him we reap benefits from His hand. If we sow sparingly we will reap sparingly. If we sow bountifully we will reap bountifully. So, "There is that scattereth and yet increaseth; and there is that withholdeth more than is meet [more than is right], but it tendeth to proverty."

We might do well to examine our own financial situation in the light of these promises. Could it be that we lack because we have not shared as we should with the Lord? Some would argue, of course, that if they had a little more, they could give. But God's principle of giving is for us to first give a portion of what we receive and not wait until we have a certain amount of income before we begin to give. The Lord does not expect large gifts from those who cannot give them. "As a man purposeth in his heart," the Scripture says, "so let him give." Proportionate giving is the New Testament standard. Some speak of tithing and this is a good principle, though even in Old Testament days giving to the Lord's work went beyond the tithe.

We must not lose sight of the truth that we are seeking to follow through to its logical conclusion. It is this: "Let him that is taught in the word communicate [share with] unto him that teacheth in all good things" (Gal. 6:6). By being obedient here we will show how we love the Lord and are under the control of the Holy Spirit. Such obedience shows that we are letting the same mind be in us that was in Christ Jesus. This is possible because the same Holy Spirit who led the Lord Jesus Christ is indwelling us and forming Christ in us.

To sow to the flesh is to reap corruption, but to sow to the Spirit is to reap life everlasting. So we must not be weary in well doing but, "As we have therefore opportunity, let us do good unto all men, especially unto them who are of the household of faith" (Gal. 6:10).

CHAPTER TWENTY-ONE

EXULTING IN THE NEW LIFE IN CHRIST

"As many as desire to make a fair shew in the flesh, they constrain you to be circumcised; only lest they should suffer persecution for the cross of Christ. For neither they themselves who are circumcised keep the law; but desire to have you circumcised, that they may glory in your flesh" (Gal. 5:12,13).

Paul's concern for the Galatian believers is seen all through this brief Epistle. At the end of it as at its beginning, he did not hesitate to expose the character and motives of the false teachers who had brought in a false gospel. They sought to avoid the stigma of the cross and at the same time taught doctrines intended to bring honor and glory to themselves.

It was in contrast to this that Paul stated: "But God forbid that I should glory, save in the cross of our Lord Jesus Christ, by whom the world is crucified unto me, and I unto the world" (Gal. 6:14). Paul's decision to glory only in the cross of Christ was made long before he ever wrote this letter to the Galatians. He called on the believers in Galatia however to take their stand with him, for only in this way would they fulfill the purposes of God in their lives.

It reminds us of Joshua in his farewell address to the people of Israel. At the climax of it he said, "Now therefore fear the Lord, and serve him in sincerity and in truth: . . . choose you this day whom ye will serve; . . . as for me and my house, we will serve the Lord" (Josh. 24:14,15). Joshua made his decision for himself and his family and then put that same decision before the people of Israel. We can thank God for Joshua's faithfulness, for the people of Israel walked in the nurture of the Lord as long as Joshua and other leaders who were his contemporaries lived among them.

In the Book of Hebrews the writer gives a similar exhortation after telling of the great revelation concerning Jesus Christ, the Redeemer and Creator who is now exalted at God's right hand: "Therefore we [Christians] ought to give more earnest heed to the things which we have heard, lest at any time we should let them slip" (Heb. 2:1). This book you are reading is, up to this point, a condensation of some 39 radio messages concerning God's grace, the working of the Holy Spirit, and the contrast of the workings of the flesh and the fruit of the Spirit. We now ought to give heed to these things.

We quote again from Hebrews: "For if the word spoken by angels was stedfast, and every transgression and disobedience received a just recompence of reward; How shall we escape, if we neglect so great salvation. . .?" (Heb. 2:3) Too many people have bypassed this verse by applying it to the unsaved. There is certainly an application to them, for they cannot escape the judgment of God if they do not apply God's salvation to themselves. The whole Book of Hebrews is written to the children of God, consequently the greatness of salvation covers more than just salvation from the condemnation of sin and providing righteousness before God. The present aspect of it deals with deliverance from the slavery of sin in the daily life. We cannot afford to neglect this aspect of it.

The Cross, the Place of Death

Let us do as Paul did and "glory in the cross of our Lord Jesus Christ." The "cross" in this context goes beyond the piece of wood on which Christ was crucified and refers to Christ's death for us. It covers His whole redemptive work. It speaks of Christ who died and rose again. From this we see then that Christ's death is the basis for victory in the daily life of each Christian. It was at the cross the world was crucified unto me and I unto the world. This is a total salvation. Our position of separation rests on the world's crucifixion to us and our victory over self rests in our crucifixion to the world.

The cross is the place of death, and being the place of death it is the place of separation. It is first of all separation from sin's condemnation which is part of the first phase of salvation. It is also separation from sin's allurements which is a day by day effect of the crucifixion. Separation from the condemnation of sin is a once-for-all result, but separation from the allurements of sin is a daily matter. The cross separates us from sin's slavery.

A Way to Life

It is remarkable to realize that the crucifixion is a way of life, not just a way of death. Christ's crucifixion was not the end of His redemptive work, for He arose from the grave and provided us with the resurrection life. Romans 6:7 says, "But he that is dead [has died] is freed from sin." This means that the person who has died is free from the claims, power, slavery and the allurements of sin. Then in verse 8 we read that if we be dead with Christ, and this should be in the past tense: "If we have died with Christ, we believe that we should also live with him: Knowing that Christ being raised from the dead dieth no more; death hath no more dominion over him. For in that he died, he died unto sin once: but in that he liveth, he liveth unto God. Likewise reckon ye yourselves to be dead [to have died] indeed unto sin, but alive unto God through Jesus Christ our Lord" (vv. 8-11). This is a glorious truth that was given not only for our learning but to help us grow in the knowledge and grace of Christ.

The great doctrinal truths in the Scriptures have their practical meaning and application for us in our daily living. Paul wrote to the Colossians: "If ye then [since ye then] be risen with Christ, seek those things which are above, where Christ sitteth at the right hand of God" (3:1). Christ died, was buried, has been raised and is now at God's right hand. He will never die again. You and I have died to sin through Christ. The Apostle admonishes us to make this effective in our day-by-day experience by seeking those things which are above.

He continues: "Set your mind on things that are above, not on the things that are upon the earth. For ye died, and your life is hid with Christ in God" (Col. 3:2,3 ARV). So this whole matter is brought before us as a decision that we must make. It is one to make now, not later on in our Christian experience.

Basis for Glorying

The basis for Paul's glorying is the cross of Christ. The Judaizers had sought their own glory but this led only to failure. The kind of self-life they lived through imposing rules and regulations ended in accomplishments which produced self-glory. But all of these self-accomplishments were reached in the sphere of the flesh nature and therefore ended in pride. This has always been a danger facing Christians, and it is no less today. There is too much Christian life and testimony on a fleshly level.

Paul's boast and joy and delight was in the One whom the world had crucified. God set His hand of approval on His Son who was crucified by raising Him from the dead.

The Cross Reveals God's Love

The cross of Christ reveals the great love of God for us. John wrote concerning this: "Herein is love, not that we loved God, but that he loved us, and sent his Son to be the propitiation for our sins" (I John 4:10). There are some who would tell us that if we would be saved we must love God. This is often the answer persons will give us when we ask if they are saved. They tell us quite readily, "I love God." But the fact is, we do not love God in order to be saved. It only comes as the result of our being saved. God loved us when we didn't love Him, loving us so much that He provided salvation for us. He loved us while we were yet sinners and enemies. When man did his worst by crucifying Christ, God did His best. So like Paul we glory in God's love.

Crucified With Christ

The cross of Christ also reveals that we have been crucified with Christ. This is what we read in Galatians 2:20: "I am crucified with Christ." I was crucified with Him therefore I am crucified with Him and the benefits of that crucifixion are with me now. So in glorying in the cross we recognize and accept the cross of Christ as our cross because when He died we died with Him.

When I recognize the fact that I have died with Christ, I accept His death as my death. I take my place with Him as one who has died to the world, to sin and to self. And because He is risen I too live. "Yet not I, but Christ liveth in me." When we are baptized, we confess that we have died with Jesus Christ and that we have been raised again to new life.

We must make a decision with regard to these things. We must appropriate this fact for ourselves. In order to make it effective in our daily living we must believe it, knowing that we have died with Christ unto sin and are now alive so that we might live righteously. Let us do it now.

The late Dr. Ironside tells of a young girl who was invited to an evening of ungodly amusement. She said to the friend who invited her, "I cannot go to such places." But the friend came back at her with this: "Many times before you've gone with me to such places."

Her answer was, "I did, but now I have buried the girl that used to go to such places, and it is no more I, but Christ who lives in me."

Have you had a funeral service for the old self? Have you come to the place of definite decision in which you have said, "I have died to the old self and to the world"? If not, as you read this make that decision and have a funeral service for the old self-life. Do not delay. There is no better time then the present for such a decision. One of the great sins of the Christian is indecision.

Israel, as you will recall, was enslaved in Egypt. When the Israelites left that land, the Red Sea to them became the point of separation from Egypt. It was there they died to Egypt and Egypt to them. It reminds us of what Paul said in II Corinthians 5:17: "Therefore if any man be in Christ, . . . old things are passed away; behold, all things are become new."

Yes, indeed, the world is crucified to me and I am crucified to the world.

The Apostle John wrote: "For whatsoever is born of God overcometh the world: and this is the victory that overcometh the world, even our faith. Who is he that overcometh the world, but he that believeth that Jesus is the Son of God?" (I John 5:4,5).

Christ "gave himself for our sins, that he might deliver us from this present evil world" according to Galatians 1:4. He said in John 16:33 that He had overcome the world. He triumphed over its selfishness, greed, hatred, slander, and persecution. He met all of it with patience, meekness and gentleness. The world gave Him a cross but He bore it because of "the joy that was set before him" (Heb. 12:2). His death was not a defeat but a triumph over death and Satan (Heb. 2:14,15). Why should we continue to grieve His heart by persisting in living in conformity to a world that crucified Him? Since Christ indwells us who believe in Him, let us, like Paul, glory in the cross of Jesus Christ by which we are crucified unto the world and the world unto us.

God Wants a Separated People

The cross, as we have seen, is a place of separation. God works on this principle of separation. He has made it basic to all Christian living and blessing. We often pray, "God bless us," but He will answer in the affirmative only if we meet His conditions. Basic to receiving His blessing is the need for living the life of separation. The power of God is released on our behalf when we live a separated life in the sense He means. There is real peril to our souls when we do not exercise by faith this separation as He wants us to.

In the Book of Genesis, very close to its beginning, we find God laid down the principle that His people were to be a separated people. After Adam and Eve sinned and Seth was born, men began to call upon the Name of the Lord (Gen. 4:26). But these were not the only people in the world. Cain, the outcast, also became the father of a considerable progeny, and eventually these two groups intermarried. We read in

Genesis 6: "And it came to pass, when men began to multiply on the face of the earth, and daughters were born unto them, That the sons of God saw the daughters of men that they were fair; and they took them wives of all which they chose. And the Lord said, My spirit shall not always strive with man, for that he also is flesh" (vv. 1-3).

The end result of these intermarriages between the godly line of Seth and the ungodly line of Cain was overwhelming evil which brought the judgment of the flood. Then God started over with Noah and his children.

Abraham Separated

The same principle is seen in the life of Abraham. Before he could be blessed he had to be separated. The Lord said to him, "Now the Lord had said unto Abram, Get thee out of thy country, and from thy kindred, and from thy father's house, unto a land that I will shew thee: And I will make of thee a great nation, and I will bless thee, and make thy name great; and thou shalt be a blessing" (Gen. 12:1,2). Abraham obeyed God only up to a point. There was not complete separation at that time.

First of all, he took Terah, his father with him. God would not let Abraham go into the land but stopped the families in Haran where they lived for 15 years until Terah died.

When Abraham departed from Haran, Lot went with him. Abraham was allowed to enter the land, but God's fullest blessing did not come until he was separated from Lot. There came at a later time strife between Lot's herdsmen and Abraham's herdsmen. So something had to give.

Abraham realized then what the problem was and said to Lot: "Separate thyself, I pray thee . . . and Lot lifted up his eyes . . . then Lot chose him all the plain of Jordan; and Lot journeyed east: and they separated themselves the one from the other" (Gen. 13:9-11).

Now God does not necessarily call all of us to complete separation from loved ones, but in Abraham's case He did.

There are other kinds of separation, however, that all of us are called upon to make. We are to be separated from the world in the sense of not following its practices and philosophies. Lot was a worldling even though he was a believer. We are told in the New Testament that the sins in Sodom and Gomorrah vexed his righteous soul day after day, but it took a catastrophe to separate him from Sodom.

God promised Abraham after he and Lot had separated: "Lift up now thine eyes, and look from the place where thou art northward, and southward, and eastward, and westward: For all the land which thou seest, to thee will I give it, and to thy seed for ever. And I will make thy seed as the dust of the earth" (Gen. 13:14-16).

Israel Separated

The same truth is seen in God's dealing with Israel. He called them out from among the nations to be a special people for Himself and then He called them forth from Egypt which is a type of the world. The Israelites were not in a position to do the will of God until they had separated from Egypt. Solomon in his dedicatory prayer made reference to this special separation by God when he said, "For thou didst separate them [Israel] from among all the people of the earth, to be thine inheritance" (I Kings 8:53). The sad fact is the people of Israel did not for very long maintain this attitude and position of separation.

Moses commented on God's dealing with Israel and their waywardness in his farewell song to the nation. Beginning with verse 8 of Deuteronomy 32 Moses told how the Most High divided the nations and set the bounds of the people according to the number of the children of Israel. He says that God found Israel in a desert land and in the waste howling wilderness and led him about and instructed him and kept him as the apple of His eye. God alone led Israel at this time and made the nation to ride on the high places of the earth. They ate the increase of the fields and, in the language of Scripture, God made them "to suck honey out of the rock, and oil out of the flinty rock" (v. 13).

But Israel was not satisfied. The people did not stay

separated. We learn in verse 15: "But Jeshurun [a poetical title for Israel under ideal conditions] waxed fat, and kicked: thou art waxen fat, thou art grown thick, thou art covered with fatness; then he forsook God which made him, and lightly esteemed the Rock of his salvation." They began to worship strange gods; they sacrificed to demons, and God said of Israel: "I will hide my face from them, I will see what their end shall be: for they are a very froward generation, children in whom is no faith" (v. 20). In the years of their plenty they became rebellious and dissatisfied. They broke the line of separation between them and their heathen neighbors. God was forced to chastise His children.

The study of the Books of Joshua, Judges and Kings shows that as long as Israel was separated to God they prospered. When they separated from Him He forsook them. The nation's ups and downs can be measured by their either adhering to separation or departing from it. It finally led to the dispersion of the Northern nation and the Babylonian captivity of the rest.

In it all God was faithful, for He said, "I sent you my messengers to bring you back, but ye mocked my messengers." So He brought up against them the kings of the Chaldeans and took away the land from His people.

We Are to Be Separated

The principles involved in this bit of ancient history are just as vital today as then. In His intercessory prayer in John 17 the Lord Jesus mentions some 6 times that believers are given to Him out of the world. In verse 6 He says to the Father: "I have manifested thy name unto the men which thou gavest me out of the world: thine they were, and thou gavest them me; and they have kept thy word." The primary reference here, of course, is to the Disciples. In verse 14 our Saviour said, "They are not of the world." Then in verse 15 He prays that the Father would not take the disciples out of the world but that they should be kept from the evil in it. In verse 18 the Saviour draws a parallel. He says, "As thou hast sent me into the world, even so have I also sent them into the world."

For what purpose? For the purpose of separation unto God. This is clear from verse 19: "And for their sakes I sanctify myself, that they also might be sanctified through the truth." The word "sanctification" means "separation."

The fact to us, then, is that we have been left in the world to demonstrate the power of the indwelling Christ to those around us. If this were not the case, the best thing would be for the Lord to call us home the moment we are saved. God has a very definite purpose for each one of us, but it can be realized only as we live separated lives.

In this same 17th chapter of John the Saviour continues defining the purposes of God with reference to the believer being left in the world. He says, "That they all may be one; as thou, Father, art in me, and I in thee, that they also may be one in us: that the world may believe that thou hast sent me. And the glory which thou gavest me I have given them; that they may be one, even as we are one: I in them, and thou in me, that they may be made perfect [mature] in one; and that the world may know that thou hast sent me, and hast loved them, as thou hast loved me" (vv. 21-23). The oneness that is spoken of in this passage is not the ecumenical oneness we hear so much about today. Man's plans in the ecumenical movement is for one big organization to include all churches. But they have left out God's plan which includes Christ and His atonement, so the movement cannot have God's blessing. The oneness spoken of is the oneness of believers in Christ. We are made members of the same Body through faith in the Saviour. But do we know through our own experience the separation involved in this unity of the Spirit?

Such a life of separation is not possible to any of us if we are to live it through the self-life. There will be nothing but failure as a result. We have this assurance, however, that God works in us both to will and to do of His good pleasure (Phil. 2:13). Or, coming back again to Galatians 6:14, we are reminded that we are crucified to the world and the world crucified to us. This is the basis and the power of this unique separation.

The cross of Jesus Christ, which means the death of Jesus Christ and I with Him, stands between me and the world. When Christ died something happened to me and something happened to the world. The bond of responsiveness between us was broken. Once the world had me in its grasp—eyes, ears, every part of me. But now that I have died with Christ on the cross, for I am crucified with Him, there is a new life. This is a new "I" which is not "I" but Christ living in me. My life is lived on a higher plane. I live in a different sphere. Crucifixion broke my bondage to the world, and the resurrection that followed gave me life and liberty in Christ Jesus. I died with Him but He lives in me. He makes His cross, that is His death, operative in me, and by living in me brings about this separation. The result is that I am separated from the world, separated unto Him.

CHAPTER TWENTY-TWO

THE CROSS MAKES THE DIFFERENCE

Men and nations seem to be constantly at each others throats trying to see who can be supreme. The same disposition is seen in the prideful way man divides society up into different classes. In reality, as far as God is concerned, there are only two classes of people in the world. And the cross of Christ makes the dividing point. There are those who are saved and those who are lost. The bond of responsiveness has been broken between the world and the person who is joined with Jesus Christ. The crucifixion and the resurrection that followed makes it possible for each believer to live on a higher plane and to move in an entirely different sphere of life. We are at liberty, those of us who trust in Christ, to live free from sin and to act in righteousness. This of course is only possible as we are under His control and as we allow the cross of the Lord Jesus Christ to be operative in us for separation.

The old and the new life are contrary to each other. The flesh strives against the Spirit and the Spirit against the flesh. It is the cross of Christ that makes the difference. Thank God, we have the Holy Spirit to enable us to be the kind of Christians we ought to be!

This change that has taken place means that I will go where I want to go and will please God in this. The reason is that it is God who works in us both to will and to do of His good pleasure. When the fallen nature in us tries to entice us to sin, the Spirit of God provides us with power to break its hold on our lives. Because we are new creatures in Christ

Jesus, our desires are new and our wants are new. This is not just something that should be, it is something that is so because we are indwelt by the Holy Spirit who is forming Christ in us.

Folly of Friendship With the World

It is possible, of course, for a believer to so oppose the Holy Spirit that finally the believer's conscience becomes calloused. The Bible speaks of those whose consciences are branded as with a hot iron. Such a Christian is hardly responsive to the dealing of the Spirit of God at all. This is dangerous. The fault lies with us for not living a separated life.

It sometimes takes the vivid language of an inspired writer like James to shock us into the realization of how wrong we can be when we are not submissive to the Spirit of God. For us to be friends of the world is to go against God. James wrote: "Ye adulterers and adulteresses, know ye not that the friendship of the world is enmity with God? whosoever therefore will be a friend of the world is the enemy of God." These words are addressed to Christians. James is writing to born again individuals. We consider the sin of adultery to be one of the most horrible sins against the institution of the family. It is a sin which puts a tremendous breach between the husband and his wife. It breaks fellowship, brings in suspicion and takes peace from the home.

James uses the figure of physical adultery to point up the awful sin of spiritual adultery. As children of God we have been married to another, even Christ. When we who have been delivered from the world become friendly again with the world, we commit spiritual adultery in God's sight. The world is the enemy of God and of Christ, and so to be its friend is an abomination to God. It was the world that nailed Christ to the cross. If He were here today, the world would do it again. We are not of the world. We have been delivered from it. It is hostile to God. There can be no neutral position for us between God and the world. We must take our stand in separation and go with the Lord.

Influence on the Christian

The influence of the cross of Christ upon the Christian is beautifully expressed in a hymn written by John Newton, a one-time merchant in slaves. He wrote:

I saw One hanging on a tree,
In agony and blood;
He turned His loving eyes on me,
As near His cross I stood.

Sure, never, till my latest breath,
Can I forget that look:
It seemed to charge me with His death,
Tho' not a word He spoke.

My conscience felt and owned the guilt,
And plunged me in despair;
I saw my sins His blood had spilt
And helped to nail Him there.

Alas! I knew not what I did—
But now my tears are vain:
Where shall my trembling soul be hid?
For I the Lord have slain.

This is what we did, and it is from the guilt of this thing that the cross has separated us. Why then should we be friendly once more with the world that crucified, yes, murdered our Lord?

Another great hymn of the cross was written by Isaac Watts:

When I survey the wondrous cross,
On which the Prince of Glory died,
All earthly gain I count but loss,
And pour contempt on all my pride.

Forbid it, Lord, that I should boast,
Save in the death of Christ, my God;
All the vain things that charm me most,
I sacrifice them to His blood.

See, from His head, His hands, His feet,
Sorrow and love flow mingled down;
Did e'er such love and sorrow meet,
Or thorns compose so rich a crown?

Were the whole realm of nature mine,
That were a present far too small;
Love so amazing, so divine,
Shall have my soul, my life, my all.

Someone has added these words:

It was on the cross He shed His blood,
It was there He was crucified,
But He rose again, and lives in my heart,
Where all is peace and perfect love.

In the light of the cross, something far deeper and more far reaching than mere external religious exercises are needed. This is why Paul states in Galatians 6:15: "For in Christ Jesus neither circumcision availeth any thing, nor uncircumcision, but a new creature." The subject of circumcision is not a controversial religious matter among believers today, but it was in the early Church. However, there are other subjects that are raised among believers that entangle them with legalism just as greatly as did the subject of circumcision. The only thing that counts in God's eyes is a new creation in Christ Jesus. The same emphasis was given in chapter 5. Verse 6 says, "For in Jesus Christ neither circumcision availeth any thing, nor uncircumcision; but faith which worketh by love." This is God's answer—faith in Christ who died for us.

Then in verse 16 we are told: "And as many as walk according to this rule, peace be on them, and mercy, and upon the Israel of God." This is the promise of peace to those who walk in the Spirit. How we need that in this day when there is hardly any peace to be found on this earth. We are living in a world of trouble, but we can walk as people with an inward calm if we follow the admonition of these various scriptures. We need to take on enough spiritual food so we can walk uprightly with our Lord.

If I did not have Christ as Saviour, and if I did not have the peace of mind promised the believer who walks with the Lord, and yet had a knowledge of what is coming on this earth in a very short time, I believe I would go to pieces. The world does not know which way to turn; but, thank God, we who know the Lord have the answer through the Word. Our Saviour's promise is: "These things I have spoken unto you, that in me ye might have peace. In this world ye shall have tribulation: but be of good cheer; I have overcome the world" (John 16:33).

Being in Christ, as we are through faith in Him, we have overcome the world. So present world conditions need not disturb us. It is true that men can take our physical life, but they cannot rob us of eternal life. In recent years we have on several occasions read and heard of missionaries of the cross who have suddenly been ushered into God's presence, their lives having been taken by God's enemies. Others under the same circumstances have been spared and have witnessed to the wonderful peace that God gave. Our Lord's promise is still true: "Peace I leave with you, my peace I give unto you: not as the world giveth, give I unto you. Let not your heart be troubled, neither let it be afraid" (John 14:27). Men talk a great deal about peace these days but the Saviour promises His peace to His child. This is the peace of God that passes all understanding.

CHAPTER TWENTY-THREE

BRAND MARKS

Paul deals with another subject in verse 17 of Galatians 6. He says, "From henceforth let no man trouble me: for I bear in my body the marks of the Lord Jesus." Paul knew where he stood. The brands or the marks of Jesus Christ were upon him.

The reference here is to a brand that could be placed on an animal or, as was often the case, the brand a slave master placed upon his slave. Paul was saying that he was the bond slave of Jesus Christ and the brand marks of the Lord were on his body.

Do we bear the marks of our Lord? It may cost some comfort and cause testings and even persecution, but no higher goal could we seek than expressed here by Paul.

The Birth Mark

What are some of the marks we should carry? There is one that we might call the birth mark. It is not something that is seen outwardly. It is not seen in the flesh body. It has to do with our spiritual birth which is a birth of royalty. We belong to the royal family of heaven because we belong to Christ. We behave differently because we are different. Through the new birth we have been made different persons. According to Colossians 1:13 God has "delivered us from the power of darkness, and translated us into the kingdom of his dear Son." We have been taken from the kingdom of the world and put into the kingdom of God's Son. This is the first mark. Do you wear it?

A New Standing

The second brand mark is that we have a new standing with God. The Bible tells us that we have been justified by faith. Justification means more than not being condemned. It means that we are declared righteous in God's sight. The impregnable strength of this position is stated for us in Romans 8:33: "Who can lay anything to the charge of God's elect? It is God that justifieth. Who is he that condemneth? It is Christ that died, yea, rather, that is risen again, who is even at the right hand of God, who also maketh intercession for us." Since we have this new standing with God we do not have to fear what the future may hold.

The world is not kind to Christians. God's people are suffering in many countries for no other reason than that they are believers in Christ. What if that should be our lot? What if we are killed for Jesus' sake? We have nothing to fear. There is no condemnation. We are righteous in God's sight.

New Resources

The third mark is a mark of new resources. This is something that no religion offers. Only true Christianity offers them. The Bible reveals what God has provided for the Christian—unlimited resources through Christ. The life we now live in the flesh we live by the faithfulness of the Son of God who loved us and gave Himself for us. A Christian is never let down by God. We can count on Him to stand by us, for He has promised never to leave us nor forsake us (Heb. 13:5).

There was a time when Jeremiah thought the Lord had let him down. He complained because he was being persecuted, but the Lord admonished him not to let the actions of the people influence him. No matter what happened to him God would stand by; consequently he was instructed to go without fear and speak what God had given him to say.

When Paul was dismayed and puzzled because of a thorn in the flesh the Lord encouraged him. He did not encourage Paul by saying He would remove the thorn. The thorn was good for Paul, but God did not let him down. He promised: "My grace is sufficient for thee." We too, need to encourage ourselves in the promises of Scripture, one of which is very outstanding in this connection: "God is able to make all grace abound toward you; that ye, always having all sufficiency in all things, may abound unto every good work" (II Cor. 9:8).

The Lord Jesus stated in the Great Commission that all power and authority was invested in Him and that He was sending us forth and would be with us unto the end of the age. This is a staggering truth to say the least. We also read in Colossians 1:29 that the Lord works mightily in us. We are admonished in Ephesians 6:10 to be strong in the Lord and in the power of His might. Think what this means! The Lord who created the heavens and the earth and who now controls them and holds them in His hand tells us to be strong in His might and in His power. What unlimited resources are ours!

Someone has said, "Our efficiency without God's sufficiency is only deficiency." This is well to remember in the light of God's promises of His power in place of our weakness.

A New Position

A fourth brand mark is that we have a new position. We are free men as the Saviour said, "If the Son shall make you free, ye shall be free indeed." This, as we have noted repeatedly, does not mean we are free to sin but we are free to do works of righteousness. We have new desires, new wants and these are all God-based and God-directed. We are admonished in this connection, to "stand fast therefore in the liberty wherewith Christ hath made us free, and be not entangled again with the yoke of bondage" (Gal. 5:1). We were entangled as slaves in sin by the old flesh nature but now we have been set free in Christ.

We are free from the fears and forebodings of men. There is no need for us to be caught up in the world's worries. We should be worry-free, for as Philippians 4:6,7 tells us we need "be careful [anxious] for nothing." We are not to worry about anything but in everything by prayer and supplication with thanksgiving we are to make our requests known unto God. Then the peace of God which passes all understanding will keep our hearts and minds through Christ Jesus. The Lord tells us that in this world we will have trouble and persecution but said our Lord, "Be of good cheer, I have overcome the world."

A New Occupation

The fifth mark of brand is that we have a new occupation. There is a new supreme goal in our lives. There is something in our hearts that causes us to want to show in our lives the fruit of the Spirit. This is not a matter of our showing off what we are, or reaching a goal of some self-attainment. Rather, it is us letting our light shine before men that God our Father may be glorified in heaven (Matt. 5:16).

The fact that we are saved means that a new light has been ignited, so we should let it shine wherever we are.

In this new occupation we have also become new producers of spiritual lives. This is soul winning. The Lord Jesus said in John 15:16: "Ye have not chosen me, but I have chosen you, and ordained you, that ye should go and bring forth fruit, and that your fruit should remain." We are born to reproduce.

These are wonderful marks that we have in Christ Jesus. No wonder Paul said that no one should bother him any more. They had no right to challenge his apostolic authority and calling. He bore ample evidence of Christ's lordship and mastership over him.

CHAPTER TWENTY-FOUR

FOUR PRACTICAL SUGGESTIONS

In concluding these studies let us look again briefly at four very practical suggestions. *The life of victory in Christ is possible only as we show continuous cooperation through faith with the Holy Spirit.* There is no once-for-all decision that removes the flesh nature from us or makes it so that we do not sin again. Salvation itself is a once-for-all matter, but just as our human birth was once for all, there followed physical growth step by step and day by day. So is it also in the spiritual realm. It is in this daily living that we should repudiate every prompting of the self-nature. We should say NO to it but not argue with it. Let us not try to resist these temptations in our own strength but let us commit ourselves to God, saying YES to Him. In the words of Psalm 37:5: "Commit thy way unto the Lord; trust also in him; and he shall bring it to pass." When we resist the attacks of Satan in the Name of Jesus Christ, the enemy will flee (Jas. 4:7).

Paul says in I Corinthians 15:31, "I die daily." The Lord Jesus stated the same truth in another way when He said in Luke 9:23: "If any man will come after me, let him deny himself, and take up his cross daily, and follow me." We have no further debt to the flesh. Let us repudiate it. This is the first practical thing to remember.

The second one is to refuse any claim of the world. The world has no claim on us as believers because we have been crucified to the world and the world to us. We are not of the world any longer. There is no point in arguing these things in our hearts. The Word is plain. Let us not give place to sin so that it reigns in our mortal bodies. It is our decision to make, so let us say NO to the flesh and to the world.

The third practical matter is that we turn to the Lord

and ask His help. At all times let us commit our ways to Him and trust Him. Let us yield our bodies to Him as Romans 12:1 admonishes us to do. Let us take of the life that He gives and live by the faithfulness of the Son of God.

In the fourth place, and this is final, let us keep a clear channel between ourselves and Christ at all times. There is not one of us who is so strong that he does not need to depend every moment upon Christ. God does not want us to sin. In fact we have noted this several times: "My little children, these things write I unto you, that ye sin not" (I John 2:1). However, when we do sin, "we have an advocate with the father, Jesus Christ the righteous." Then let us confess our sins and since He is faithful and just He will forgive us our sins and cleanse us from all unrighteousness (I John 1:9).

There is no need to become moody or depressed over having sinned since we know the remedy and the way back into fellowship. We will undoubtedly fail many times; but let us come to the Lord in true repentance and He will forgive us. He knows our weakness and delights when we come to claim His strength and power.

Infinite power is at hand for us to use. God wants us to ask Him for it and to appropriate it every day and moment of our lives.

Conclusion of the Letter

The Apostle Paul closed the Galatian Epistle with a brief, pointed sentence. He said, "Brethren, the grace of our Lord Jesus Christ be with your spirit. Amen" (6:18). In the original the word "brethren" or "brothers" is last in the sentence. "Grace" is first. The Galatians were saved by grace and kept by grace. Their day by day victory was based on grace. In the words of Peter, they were to "grow in grace." Grace did for them what the Law could not do and was never intended by God to do.

So it is with us. By faith we have access into grace, that is into God's favor in which we stand securely (Rom. 5:2). Our ministry is to testify to the gospel of the grace of God (Acts 20:24). We work for the Lord according to the grace He gives us (Rom. 12:3,6). Any good in us and any good we accomplish for the Lord is due to His grace (I Cor. 15:10).

It is grace that teaches us to deny ungodliness and worldly lusts and to live seriously, uprightly and godly in this present evil world. And it is grace that teaches us to look for the glorious appearing of Jesus Christ our great God and Saviour (Titus 2:11-13).

It was grace that kept intact the spiritual brotherhood between Paul and the Galatian believers. The severe things he had to write to them did not change the fact that they were "brethren." It is the same grace that binds the family of God together in our day. May the rivers of God's grace continue to flow among us.

> *Amazing grace, how sweet the sound,*
> *That saved a wretch like me!*
> *I once was lost, but now am found;*
> *Was blind, but now I see.*
>
> *'Twas grace that taught my heart to fear,*
> *And grace my fears relieved;*
> *How precious did that grace appear,*
> *The hour I first believed.*
>
> *Thro' many dangers, toils, and snares,*
> *I have already come;*
> *'Tis grace that brought me safe thus far,*
> *And grace will lead me home.*